OSPREY AIRCRAFT OF THE ACES • 101

Luftwaffe *Viermot* Aces 1942–45

SERIES EDITOR: TONY HOLMES
OSPREY AIRCRAFT OF THE ACES • 101

Luftwaffe *Viermot* Aces 1942–45

Robert Forsyth

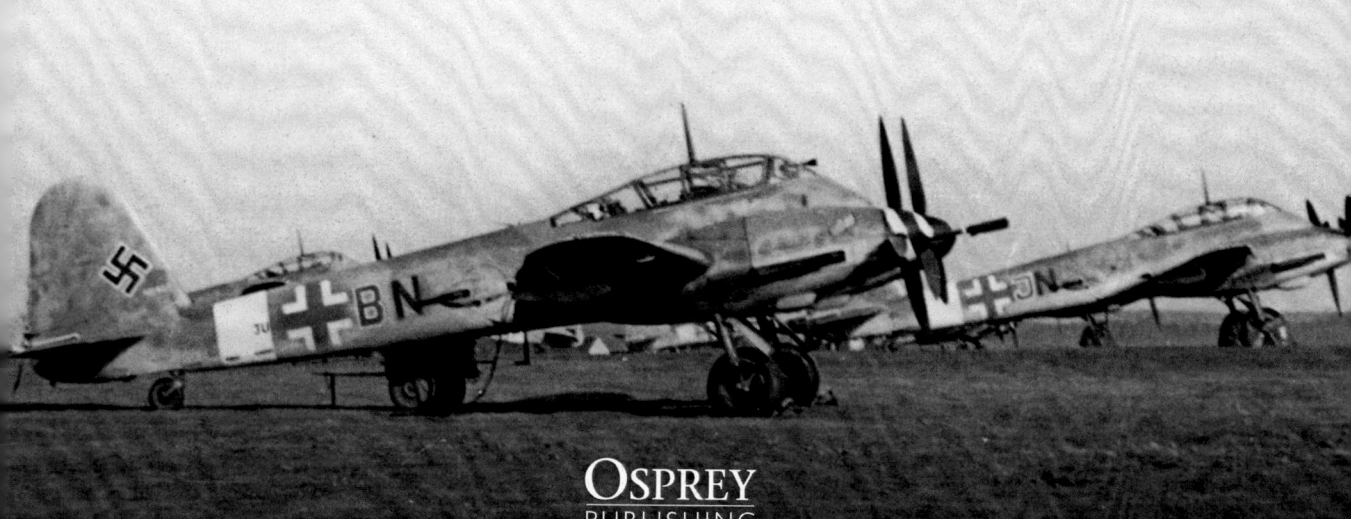

OSPREY
PUBLISHING

Front Cover

On 1 August 1943, a combined force of B-24 Liberators drawn from five groups of the US Eighth and Ninth Air Forces launched a major strike on the Ploesti oilfields and refinery complex north of Bucharest, in Rumania, which produced some ten million tons of oil per year, with the aim of depriving the Third Reich of a valued source of fuel. Flying from bases near Benghazi, in Libya, the 178 B-24s constituting Operation *Tidal Wave* followed a 2000-mile course across the Mediterranean, passing over the island of Corfu, before turning at the Albanian coast and heading inland over Yugoslavia and Bulgaria towards the target. The bombers, flying at low level, were harried by flak and fighters.

Mark Postlethwaite's dramatic, cover art depicts the moment that Feldwebel Albert Palm of 3./JG 4 manoeuvred his Bf 109G-2 'Yellow 6' to attack a B-24 of the 44th BG – the 'Flying Eightballs' – by diving from astern as the low-flying bombers emerged from the drifting clouds of black smoke spiralling up from the burning refineries.

3./JG 4, under the command of the combat-seasoned Hauptmann Manfred Spenner (formerly of JG 52) and based at Mizil, northeast of Ploesti, had been formed in Rumania in early January 1943 and built up with Rumanian personnel under a Luftwaffe officer cadre. The *Staffel's* prime duty at this time was the air defence of the oilfields and refineries, although the following year it relocated with the rest of I./JG 4 to western Germany to engage in the defence of the Reich.

During the bitter action over Ploesti, Alfred Palm would account for the destruction of a B-24. He had flown previously with 8./JG 77, and at the time of leaving that *Staffel* to join 3./JG 4 he had 28 victories to his credit. In March 1944 Palm suffered severe injuries to his right foot and ankle when he was forced to bail out over Italy after his Bf 109 was attacked by Kittyhawks. Once he had recovered, Palm served as an instructor, before returning to JG 4 towards the end of the war.

Thirty-three B-24s were lost to flak during the Ploesti raid and ten to fighters. Another 56 Liberators were damaged

OSPREY PUBLISHING
Bloomsbury Publishing Plc

PO Box 883, Oxford, OX1 9PL, UK
1385 Broadway, 5th Floor, New York, NY 10018, USA
Email: info@ospreypublishing.com

OSPREY is a trademark of Osprey Publishing, a division of Bloomsbury Publishing Plc

© 2011 Osprey Publishing

First published in Great Britain in 2011 by Osprey Publishing

Transferred to digital print-on-demand in 2019

Printed and bound by PrintOnDemand-Worldwide.com, Peterborough, UK

All rights reserved. Apart from any fair dealing for the purpose of private study, research, criticism or review, as permitted under the Copyright, Design and Patents Act, 1988, no part of this publication may be reproduced, stored in a retrieval system, or transmitted in any form or by any means, electronic, electrical, chemical, mechanical, optical, photocopying, recording or otherwise without prior written permission of the copyright owner. Enquiries should be addressed to the Publisher.

A CIP catalogue record for this book is available from the British Library

ISBN: 978 1 84908 438 3
e-book ISBN: 978 1 84908 439 0

Edited by Tony Holmes
Page design by Tony Truscott
Cover Artwork by Mark Postlethwaite
Aircraft Profiles by Jim Laurier
Index by Michael Forder
Originated by United Graphic Pte Ltd

The Woodland Trust
Osprey Publishing supports the Woodland Trust, the UK's leading woodland conservation charity.

www.ospreypublishing.com
To find out more about our authors and books visit our website. Here you will find extracts, author interviews, details of forthcoming events and the option to sign-up for our newsletter.

Acknowledgements

I would like to thank Erik Mombeek and Eddie J Creek for their kind and essential support to this project. I would also like to acknowledge the kind assistance of J Richard Smith, Martin Pegg, Nick Beale and Donald Nijboer.

Many years ago I interviewed and corresponded with a number of former German fighter pilots who experienced at first-hand what it was like to engage formations of heavy bombers, including Adolf Galland, Oskar Bösch, Fritz Buchholz, Richard Franz, Klaus Neumann, Willi Reschke, Gustav Rödel, Franz Steiner, Franz Stigler and Willi Unger. The information that I was able to glean from those exchanges is as important today as it was back in the late 1980s and early 1990s when I obtained it. I thank them for their patience and cooperation during my research of some 20 years ago.

This book is dedicated to David Wadman, whose cheerfulness and fortitude is an example to all. Looking back, I realise that the book has its origins in a discussion I had with Dave late one night 21 years ago in a bar in Mesa, Arizona – after one beer too many. I knew that was a mistake.

CONTENTS

CHAPTER ONE
HEAD-ON 6

CHAPTER TWO
CORNERED WOLF 20

CHAPTER THREE
'BIG WEEK' AND BERLIN 34

CHAPTER FOUR
BLOODY APRIL 45

CHAPTER FIVE
'STOVEPIPES' AND DESTROYERS 62

CHAPTER SIX
ALL-OUT DEFENCE 70

CHAPTER SEVEN
STORMBIRDS 84

APPENDICES 90
COLOUR PLATES COMMENTARY 92
INDEX 96

CHAPTER ONE

HEAD-ON

At the beginning of August 1942 the Luftwaffe fighter force was committed predominantly to two major theatres of war. To the east, *Gruppen* drawn from six *Jagdgeschwader*, fielding around 500 single-engined fighters, were operating in the USSR, deployed on a 2000-kilometre front engaging an enemy that, in terms of size, matched them. By this stage of the war the Soviet air force had recovered from setbacks it had suffered during the previous winter and spring and was enjoying a period of qualitative and organisational improvement. For the time being, as the long drive towards Stalingrad loomed, more intuitive German commanders realised that an early victory in Russia was a dim prospect.

In North Africa, a smaller force comprising six *Jagdgruppen* from two *Geschwader* provided support to the *Afrika Korps* as it struggled to break the line which the British held between El Alamein and the Qattara depression.

Thousands of kilometres away from these distant battlefronts, most of the German population in its homes and factories, in its offices and shops, its schools and hospitals, although placed on a war-footing, continued to function, in daylight hours at least, without much direct disruption from the enemy. For two years, RAF Bomber Command had mounted a determined campaign of night raids using light and medium bombers to strike at shipping, the transport infrastructure and industry in several major cities, including Berlin. In this, the British had been relatively successful. Equally, however, the Luftwaffe had built up an effective and technologically sophisticated nightfighter and flak organisation that inflicted an increasing toll on the night bombers.

In a scene typical of its time, pilots of 2./JG 2, clad in life jackets and flare bandoliers, gather around one of the unit's Fw 190A-4s at their airfield in France to be briefed by their *Staffelkapitän* in early 1943. From the summer of 1942 to mid-1943, this *Staffel*, along with the others of JG 2 and JG 26, formed the Luftwaffe's first line of defence against the Allied bomber offensive

Most of Western Europe was firmly under German occupation. In one form or another, Hitler's 'Thousand-Year Reich' spread from Norway to the French Riviera, from the Channel Coast to Czechoslovakia. Although America had joined the European war, and its first P-38 Lightning fighters and B-17 Flying Fortress heavy bombers were arriving in England, so secure did the Germans consider their hold on Europe to be that responsiblity for guarding the skies over the western 'gateway' to the occupied territories in the hours of daylight was assigned, in the main, to just two *Jagdgeschwader* (JG 2 and JG 26), based in France and Belgium.

Fundamentally, there was nothing wrong with this state of affairs. Since early 1941, the RAF had concerned itself with a 'lean towards France', mounting a campaign of offensive fighter sweeps aimed – nominally – at needling and testing the German air defences by strafing ground installations, troop concentrations, railways and airfields, although as one British historian has commented, 'the Germans appeared to be largely unimpressed'. During the Channel campaign of 1941–42, fighter pilots on both sides had learned, developed and refined fighter-versus-fighter tactics. Pitted against the RAF's Spitfires, Hurricanes and Whirlwinds were the trusty, but regularly re-engineered, Messerschmitt Bf 109Fs and, following its introduction to the Channel Front in mid-1941, the much vaunted radial-engined Focke-Wulf Fw 190A.

Flying these two fighter types, the France and Belgium-based German *jagdflieger* demonstrated impressive levels of combat dexterity, with a number of pilots from both *Geschwader* notching up high personal scores, and in doing so, becoming the darlings of the propaganda reporters and film cameras for the benefit of German newsreels 'back home'.

In Holland, another unit, JG 1, had been assigned the defence of the northwestern approaches to Germany. As with its sister units to the south, most of JG 1's activity to mid-1942 had centred upon intercepting Spitfires and probing formations of British twin-engined Bleinheims, Whitleys, Hampdens, Hudsons, Beauforts and Wellingtons (known by the Germans as *'Zweimots'* – 'two-engines'). The latter attacked shipping and coastal targets and the German ports, as well as some targets further inland, during the hours of daylight. These raids, frequently mounted without fighter escort or with an escort that was large but poorly organised (known as 'Circuses'), suffered casualties at the hands of a German defence, which was wrongly assumed to have been significantly weakened by a mass relocation to the USSR.

Between 11 November 1941 and 22 February 1942, the RAF had mounted daylight bombing operations on 20 days (543 sorties), from which 40 aircraft were lost (7.4 per cent), although the precise respective figures attributable to flak and fighters are not known.

The RAF usually despatched formations of between 10-30 bombers at a height of a little over 20,000 ft. If escorted, the fighters were ordered to remain with the bombers, much as Luftwaffe fighter pilots had been instructed to do over Britain in the summer of 1940. Initially, the Germans, under orders to attack only the bombers, and to ignore the escort, dealt with these formations by manoeuvring their fighters above and behind the bombers before diving through any escort, opening fire randomly at hastily selected targets and then diving away.

CHAPTER ONE

Guarding the airspace over Holland and the northern approaches to the Reich against Allied bombers in 1942–43 was JG 1. Here, Fw 190A-3 'White 1' of the *Staffelkapitän* of 10. *Staffel*, Oberleutnant Friedrich Eberle, is rolled back towards its dispersal by groundcrew at Bergen-op-Zoom, in Holland, in May 1942. Note the 12 victory markings on the fighter's rudder

In November 1941, the *Kommodore* of JG 26, Oberst Adolf Galland, was appointed the *General der Jagdflieger* following the untimely and unwelcome death of the previous incumbent, the revered Werner Mölders. Galland successfully pushed for a revision of the prevailing bomber interception tactics and gained more freedom for his pilots to take on the Spitfires that would pursue the Bf 109s as they broke away from their pass over the bombers.

Galland recalled the weight of fire from a Spitfire at this time as being 'very effective'. While with JG 26, his pilots had devised special tactics that saw them exploiting cloud cover to move slowly and carefully towards the British escort without being noticed, before quickly assessing a vulnerable or 'covenient' part of the formation to attack. The German pilots would then climb slightly and dive quickly before the escort had a chance to react. Galland also experimented with the method of deploying a number of his fighters to the rear of and above an enemy formation, thus diverting the attention of the escort while, alone, he would climb slowly and gradually out of the clouds below the formation. Hopefully remaining unseen, he would close in on one of the lower elements, select a target, shoot it down and then quickly dive into the clouds to get away.

Such tactics occasionally brought success, but they could also result in losses, such as on 13 October when, having attacked a formation of Blenheims from below and shot one down in flames, Galland veered away unscathed. His inexperienced wingman, however, was not so fortunate, drawing fire from the turret gunner of the Blenheim he was targeting. Leutnant Peter Göring, a nephew of Hermann Göring, crashed to his death. Also, these methods depended to a great extent on weather and an ineffective or slow-to-react escort.

Somewhat more ominous had been the appearance, in July 1941, of a new British *four*-engined bomber – a *'Viermot'* (a contraction of 'four-engines') – the Short Stirling, which carried a crew of six protected by no fewer than eight 0.303-in Browning machine guns housed in nose, dorsal and tail turrets.

On 10 July, three escorted Stirlings bombed the Chocques power station in France. Hauptmann Rolf Pingel, the *Kommandeur* of I./JG 26, a highly-experienced veteran of the Spanish Civil War and a Knight's Cross-holder with 28 victories, pursued one of them alone from France, across the English Channel, to England, where he managed to inflict damage on the Stirling's tail section, before a burst of fire from its upper gunner hit his Bf 109's engine. He was forced to descend to a lower-altitude, whereupon he was attacked by a Spitfire and had to force-land, thus presenting the British with their first largely intact Bf 109F-2.

Six Stirlings had also been used to attack the German battle cruiser *Scharnhorst* at La Pallice on 23 July, one of them tellingly, but erroneously, claiming the destruction of two Bf 109s with its defensive armament during the raid. Likewise, in an indication of already heightened awareness of what probably lay ahead in the air war, pilots of JG 2 reported the Stirlings as being 'Boeing bombers'. However, what really mattered to the Germans was that they accounted for the destruction of a Stirling when Leutnant Ulrich Adrian of 1./JG 2 shot down one of the six, thus becoming the first pilot from JG 2 – and possibly the Luftwaffe – to account for a *Viermot* destroyed.

However, despite this unique success, a freshly trained German fighter pilot joining any of the western-based fighter units could justifiably expect to be primarily engaged in combat against enemy fighters and, on occasion, light and medium British bombers, often lacking in adequate defensive armament. Although Galland noted that at this time 'the strain on the men and material of JG 2 and JG 26 was much worse than during the Battle of Britain', providing a new *jagdflieger* followed the instructions of his more senior and experienced fellow pilots, he would stand a better chance in terms of life expectancy than his colleagues flying in the USSR or North Africa. Indeed, such was the state of affairs by 17 June 1942 that the Commander-in-Chief of RAF Fighter Command, Air Vice-Marshal Sholto Douglas, whose aircraft continued to suffer from a lack of extension to their range, was forced to concede that the balance of casualties had turned against him and in favour of the Germans.

But, for the Germans, there was to be a rude shock. On 1 June, Maj Gen Henry H 'Hap' Arnold, the commanding general of the US Army Air Force, displayed an ebullient and confident mood when, having spent the previous night at the country residence of Winston Churchill on the invitation of the British Prime Minister, he cabled the US President, Franklin D Roosevelt. While at Chequers, Arnold had become aware of the effects of mass bombing following the RAF night raid on Cologne the night before, when 890 bombers had dropped more that 1450 tons of bombs on the German city, killing 469 of its residents and injuring 5027. More than 12,000 buildings were affected in some way by the raid, and water and electricity supplies, telephone

Adolf Galland, the former *Kommodore* of JG 26, was appointed *General der Jagdflieger*, in November 1941, just a few months before the USAAF commenced daylight bombing operations over Europe. Not always popular, especially with the lower ranks, Galland nevertheless placed great emphasis on honing the Luftwaffe's response to the heavy bomber threat. He is seen here in November 1943 during a visit to Achmer, where he met with Major Hans-Günther von Kornatzki (far left), commander of the newly formed *Sturmstaffel* 1, and Hauptmann Horst Geyer (far right), *Kommandoführer* of *Erprobungskommando* 25. An Fw 190 with underwing mortars can be seen behind the men

CHAPTER ONE

The wreckage of an RAF four-engined Short Stirling bomber lies in open countryside in Denmark following a minelaying operation over the Baltic in May 1942. This aircraft, belonging to No 149 Sqn, was lost during a night raid, but from the summer of 1942, RAF Bomber Command sent Stirlings, Halifaxs and Lancasters on occasional day raids, making them the first *Viermots* the Luftwaffe intercepted in daylight

communication and mail were inoperative or disrupted for two weeks. 'England is the place to win the war', proclaimed Arnold to Roosevelt. 'Get planes and troops over as soon as possible'.

This, the Americans did with considerable endeavour, and by the end of August 1942, the US Eighth Air Force's VIII Bomber Command (BC) in England had three bomb groups to its name, representing a force of 119 B-17E Flying Fortresses. The latter was an all-metal, four-engined aircraft with a range of 2000 miles, but it had been conceived essentially as a medium bomber. This meant that its range and endurance had been optimised in a trade-off with bombload, which stood at just 4000 lbs.

In terms of armament, even this early variant of the Flying Fortress was well served. The rear fuselage featured a tail turret mounting twin 0.50-in Browning machine guns for anticipated defence against fighter attack from the rear, these being hand-operated by a gunner in a sit-kneel position. Additionally, a dorsal 360 degree-turn power-operated turret was installed into the upper fuselage immediately aft of the cockpit, while a remotely controlled ventral turret, fitted with a periscope sight to be used by a gunner in a prone position, was built in under the central fuselage aft of the bomb-bay. Both these turrets also fielded twin Brownings, meaning that the B-17E was truly a 'Fortress', its crew of ten being protected by eight 0.50-in guns in total and a single 0.30-in nose-mounted gun in a framed nose cone.

The nature of the air war over Europe changed indelibly when, in the late afternoon of 17 August, 12 Flying Fortresses of the 97th BG, escorted by four squadrons of RAF Spitfire Mk IXs, bombed the marshalling yards at Sotteville, near Rouen in France, dropping 18 tons of bombs. 'Going along for the ride' as an observer was Gen Ira Eaker, commander of VIII BC. Fw 190s from II./JG 26 (whose pilots ironically identified the bombers as British Stirlings) and JG 2 launched an attack over Ypreville. Two B-17s were lightly damaged by flak rather than fighters, and there were no casualties. According to the Eighth Air Force, there were 'a few brief exchanges of fire with enemy fighters – mission successful'. Just one American gunner 'got a shot at an FW'.

Following this inaugural operation, and despite some sniping in the British press over the comparatively light bombload of the B-17 when compared with RAF bombers, as well as a perceived low speed and lack of armament, Maj Gen Carl Spaatz, the commander of the Eighth Air

Force, was pleased with initial performance and results. Indeed, he made it clear that he had no plans to substitute the Flying Fortress for any British bomber in production. His commitment to the B-17 was given some justification by Adolf Galland, who recounted to Allied interrogators shortly after the war that even in this opening phase of the battle against the *Viermots* 'the defensive power of the bombers was regarded as extremely effective, and actually instilled considerable apprehension into the minds of the fighter pilots. The actual effect of the weapons was more mental than material, and at first the German fighter pilots simply would not attack'.

Throughout the rest of August the Americans launched more tentative raids on marshalling yards, shipyards and airfields, but there was no contact of any significance between German fighters and the American bombers, although on the 20th Unteroffizier Jan Schild of 2./JG 26 claimed a 'Stirling' shot down over the Channel. The 'kill' went unconfirmed, however, and there is no reported corresponding loss of such an aircraft by the RAF. If anything, it is likely Schild damaged a Flying Fortress from the small force that bombed the Amiens marshalling yards that day.

All this changed on 6 September when Hauptmann Karl-Heinz Meyer, the *Kommandeur* of II./JG 26, became the first German fighter pilot to be credited with the destruction of a Flying Fortress when he shot down a B-17F of the 97th BG near Amiens for his tenth personal victory. The bomber had been one of a force of 51 aircraft sent by Eaker to bomb the Potez factory at Meaulte, where Bf 109s were overhauled and repaired. The Luftwaffe was presented with the opportunity to prove just how menacing it could be when the bombers failed to rendezvous with their Spitfire escort at the appointed time. The unprotected formation pressed on to Meaulte, only to be bounced by the Fw 190s of Meyer's *Gruppe*.

When the Spitfires finally caught up with the B-17s, they in turn were bounced by Fw 190s of JG 2. The accolade of the second Flying Fortress to fall to German guns went to Oberfeldwebel Willi Roth of 4./JG 26, who was credited with the shooting down of a 92nd BG aircraft after a series of attacks by at least five Fw 190s. According to the Eighth Air Force's summary of operations, the German fighters had launched attacks from 'all directions' and 'out of the sun'.

From this point onwards, the Jagdwaffe and VIII BC joined in a battle of steadily increasing attrition. In reviewing German fighter tactics against B-17s to 15 September, a USAAF technical officer reported;

'A running commentary of enemy fighter activity is kept up between the fighter cover and the first pilots of the bomber formation. The co-pilots and all other crew members of ships in the bombing formation are on the inter-phone system to give and receive information on enemy fighter attacks. Gunners are given sectors to search so that all fields of view are covered. At least three guns may be brought to bear on any point 400 yards from a B-17F. Mutual firepower from ships in formation greatly increases the number of guns that may be fired at enemy aircraft attacking the formation.

'Enemy fighter attacks from all angles have been experienced. They started with astern attacks, went to quarter, beam, below, bow and,

Mechanics and armourers attend to an early Fw 190 of 4./JG 26 at Abbeville in the summer of 1942. This *Gruppe* was one of those that bore the brunt of the Eighth Air Force's earliest incursions over France

on the last two missions, head-on attacks. The success of all these attacks has been about the same. The B-17s that have been shot down have been from the usual causes of straggling and gunners getting killed. Damage to aeroplanes returning has been slight, and there have only been two aeroplanes at any one time out of commission due to enemy gunfire.

'Gunners have caused many fighters to decide not to attack by firing a burst just as the fighter begins the turn-in to attack. This has been done on some occasions when the fighter was 1000 yards away or more.'

The foregoing indicates the still random and arbitrary style with which the *jagdflieger* were conducting their attacks on heavy bombers at this time, although Eighth Air Force crews reported that from August to November 1942 'tail attacks were the rule, and were the form of attack our bomber armament and armour plate was primarily designed to protect against'.

In the early afternoon of 23 November 1942, a force of 36 unescorted heavy bombers attacked the St Nazaire U-boat base, and this time the 28 Flying Fortresses were accompanied by eight of the recently arrived Consolidated B-24 Liberators of the 93rd BG – aircraft which were superior to the B-17 in terms of performance and bombload. Like the Boeing bomber, the B-24 bristled with defensive armament, incorporating ten or eleven 0.50-in Browning machine guns housed in nose, upper and tail turrets. As the B-17s made their bomb run, Fw 190s from Hauptmann Egon Mayer's III./JG 2 swept in to meet them.

Mayer had served with JG 2 since December 1939 and secured his first victory in June 1940 during the campaign in France. After a brief spell at the *Jagdfliegerschule* in Werneuchen, he returned to the

Geschwader in the autumn of 1940. By November 1942 (the month he was appointed to lead III./JG 2) he had been credited with 52 enemy aircraft destroyed, many of them Spitfires.

The attack provided Mayer with the perfect opportunity to test a new tactic that had been the subject of discussion among German fighter commanders for several weeks. Forming into *Ketten* of three aircraft, the Fw 190s went into attack initially from ahead and to the left. When in range, Mayer opened fire with a no-deflection burst that gave him the impression that his cone of fire was reaching the area in front of the enemy aircraft. In pulling up to the left, he observed hits in the starboard wing area of the B-17. The wing broke away and the Flying Fortress turned over and spun in, exploding as it went.

Crucially, Mayer had experienced no defensive fire as he made his approach. Following their attack, the German pilots then made sharp pulls up to the left or right and again, at first, there was no defensive fire, but this was followed by heavy fire as the Focke-Wulfs moved over or beneath and behind the bombers using a climb or half-roll.

After this initial attack several more front low passes were made against other Flying Fortresses in the formation, and on a final attack strikes were seen in the fuselage areas and wing roots. Whilst turning under one B-17 Mayer saw a 'light ball of fire' beneath the aircraft, moments after which the bomber 'spun in, twisting and turning and exploding after receiving more hits from the rear'.

Next, Mayer aimed for the B-24s, attacking one from ahead and to one side, keeping his speed as low as possible. As he opened fire on the Liberator, Mayer's Fw 190 'skidded' in the direction of flight of the bomber by applying simple rudder movement. Violent explosions were seen from the first shots, and the American bomber 'pulled up slightly and dived straight down without spinning. No one bailed out'.

Despite this success, there was a loss on the German side when one of Mayer's wingmen, Unteroffizier Theodore Angele of 7. *Staffel*, was killed over the Channel by return fire as he pulled his Fw 190 up behind the bombers after his attack – another pilot sustained heavy damage to his aircraft at a similar moment.

Following this encounter, however, Mayer believed that a frontal pass, as opposed to the customary rearward attack, offered the best chance to inflict damage on the bombers' vulnerable cockpit area. Even more importantly, the frontal arc of defensive fire was the weakest. Four bombers had gone down following the attack for the loss of one Fw 190. Indeed, as the HQ of the Eighth Air Force noted after the mission;

'A change of enemy fighter tactics was observed in this operation, nearly all attacks being frontal and apparently aimed at the right side of the nose.'

Amidst a field of wheat in France in the summer of 1943, the *Kommodore* of JG 2, Major Egon Mayer, stands on the starboard wing of a B-17F that he has shot down. In late 1942 it was Mayer, at the time *Kommandeur* of III./JG 2, who convinced Galland that a frontal pass against a B-17 offered the best chance of bringing it down. The relatively intact aircraft would have been examined and stripped of parts of tactical or technical interest and use

Engine oil is pumped from a bowser into the tank of Oberleutnant Egon Mayer's Fw 190 'White 7' of 7./JG 2 during the summer of 1942. Just visible is the *Staffel's* emblem of a thumb pressed down on a top hat

'From that moment', one historian recorded, 'the B-17 was obsolete as a self-defending bomber'.

Egon Mayer would receive the Knight's Cross in August 1941 and be credited with 102 enemy aircraft destroyed by the time he was killed in an encounter with P-47s over France on 2 March 1944. His first success against a B-17 would not be his last, and, despite his death, Mayer would remain one of the Luftwaffe's highest-scoring aces against the *Viermots*, with no fewer than 26 confirmed four-engined kills. This tally included two on 3 January 1943, a feat he repeated on 5 January 1944, followed by three B-24s and one B-17 destroyed 48 hours later.

Encouraged by Mayer's initial success, Galland issued a circular to all Luftwaffe fighter units;

'A. The attack from the rear against a four-engined bomber formation promises little success and almost always brings losses. If an attack from the rear must be carried though, it should be done from above or below, and the fuel tanks and engines should be the aiming points.

'B. The attack from the side can be effective, but it requires thorough training and good gunnery.

'C. The attack from the front, front high, or front low, all with low speed, is the most effective of all. Flying ability, good aiming and closing up to the shortest possible range are the prerequisites for success.

'Basically, the strongest weapon is the massed and repeated attack by an entire fighter formation. In such cases, the defensive fire can be weakened and the bomber formation broken up.'

Senior unit commanders issued instructions to their pilots to firstly determine a bomber formation's direction of flight, then to fly on a course parallel to and to one side of the bombers until they were about 4000-5000 metres ahead of them so that the formation could be seen over either of the horizontal stabilisers. This was usually about five to seven minutes after overtaking the formation. The pilots were then to bank around tightly with their engines throttled back, immediately after which they were to turn in by *Schwärme* and attack head-on.

During this final approach to the target, the fighters were to fly level with the bombers for the last 1400 metres, open fire at 825 metres and then get away by flying flat over the formation. The key aiming points were the cabin area of the target aircraft and the No 3 engine. In executing the head-on attack, it was calculated that, on average, it required 20 hits with 20 mm shells from an MG 151 cannon to bring down a heavy bomber. But as the fighter closed in on its target, the combined approach speed would be approximately 805 km/h at 183 metres per second, and this allowed only a half-second burst from the fighter before it would be forced to break away in order to avoid collision with the bomber. However, in practice, not many German pilots had the nerve to make their exit flat over the bombers, with most using a split-S to dive away many metres in front of the B-17s or B-24s, thus reducing firing time and shooting down fewer bombers. After a successful head-on attack the *jagdflieger* were to turn and complete the destruction of any bomber that had been knocked out of formation and isolated, or which was 'straggling'.

Despite this new doctrine – based on sound principles – German tactics against the bombers continued to sway between attacks from the rear and from head-on, although the Eighth Air Force admitted that 'from December 1942 through to the end of January 1943, nose attacks predominated – in fact on some missions no other form of attack was reported. When nose attacks became a serious threat, the nose defence of our bombers was weak'.

In cases when rearward attacks were made, however, they were to be executed in a concentration of at least *Schwarm* strength in rapid succession, from slightly high or low, with the fighters getting away flat over the formation. A diving exit behind the bombers was to be performed only if the fighter's speed was so low that a dive was necessary in order to evade defensive fire. Speed was essential, since the relative speeds of the fighters and bombers were so low that the marksmanship of the bomber gunners' was found to improve quite noticeably. Those pilots persisting in rearward attacks found that the most vulnerable spot on a bomber was the wing area between the fuselage and the in-board engines. Again, the No 3 on a B-17 was considered particularly important because it powered the hydraulics system.

USAAF crews noted that in February and March 1943, beam attacks increased (from the 'two', 'three' and 'four o'clock' and 'eight', 'nine' and 'ten o'clock' positions),

The view seen by a Luftwaffe fighter pilot as he would have approached a pair of B-17Fs for a frontal attack. Egon Mayer believed that a frontal pass, as opposed to the customary rearward attack, against heavy bombers offered the best chance to inflict damage on the vulnerable cockpit area. Even more importantly, the frontal arc of defensive fire was the weakest

while between April and June, tail attacks increased, beam attacks decreased and nose attacks 'held their own'.

However, in August 1943, the *Oberkommando der Luftwaffe* (OKL) ordered that *all* attacks were to be made from the rear, rather than by a frontal pass chiefly because a large percentage of the young pilots equipping the *Jagdgeschwader* from the fighter schools encountered difficulty in undertaking the latter type of attack. The frontal pass involved a high combined closing speed which, in turn, demanded great skill in gunnery, range estimation and flying control. The slightest evasive action on the part of the bombers made this type of attack even more difficult. In contrast, evasive action taken against attacks from the rear was thought to be ineffective. This was picked up the USAAF;

'The period from July through to December was marked by a high percentage of tail attacks and a decrease in the proportion of nose attacks.'

The gradual switch from head-on back to rear-mounted attacks was timely, as September 1943 saw the appearance of the new B-17G fitted with a twin-gun 'chin' turret in the nose. This in turn provided the Flying Fortress with the vital forward armament it needed to counter frontally-mounted attacks.

Nevertheless, there were a select few among the *jagdflieger* who demonstrated early on the 'prerequisites' of 'flying ability, good aiming' and a suitable degree of courage to enjoy noteworthy success against the *Viermots*. Included in this elite and pioneering group was Oberleutnant Josef Wurmheller, *Staffelkapitän* of 9./JG 2, who is known to have shot down two B-17s in one day over Brittany on 16 February 1943. This was, in itself, considered to have been an unusual and remarkable feat of skill and bravery.

By this date Wurmheller already had a formidable reputation, having accounted for the destruction of more than 50 Spitfires over the Channel

Following his return from a mission over the Channel coast, Oberleutnant Josef Wurmheller, *Staffelkapitän* of 9./JG 2, chats with a technical officer of his *Gruppe*. The yellow rudder of Wurmheller's Fw 190A-6 'Yellow 2' (Wk-Nr 530314) is adorned with an emblem of the Knight's Cross and a marking denoting 60 victories, a figure reached in August 1942. The second row of additional victory bars and a part of the third row – eight in all – show American stars, all of which denoted B-17s shot down

Front between September 1940 and October 1942, as well as nine Soviet aircraft while serving with 5./JG 53 in Russia in mid-1941. He had been awarded the Knight's Cross on 4 September 1941 while an oberfeldwebel with 31 victories, and the Oak Leaves followed on 13 November 1942.

During May 1943, Wurmheller shot down a further four B-17s and another three in July. He would remain with 9. *Staffel* until 8 June 1944, when he was appointed *Kommandeur* of III./JG 2 in its operations on the Normandy invasion front (replacing Hauptmann Herbert Huppertz who had been killed, having accounted for 17 *Viermots*). Fourteen days later, on 22 June, 'Sepp' Wurmheller was shot down and killed during combat with Allied fighters. His final score of four-engined bombers amounted to at least 20 out of a total of 102 victories. He had repeated his feat of knocking down two Flying Fortresses in one day on 3 September 1943 and again on the 15th of that month. Eighteen of his victories were B-17s and two were B-24s. Wurmheller was awarded the Swords to the Knight's Cross posthumously on 24 October 1944.

Standing alongside him in this early phase of operations against the 'heavies' was the redoubtable Oberleutnant Georg-Peter Eder, the *Staffelkapitän* of 12./JG 2, who was instrumental in working with Egon Mayer to develop the principle of the head-on attack. Despite being shot down and wounded in Russia, as well as having suffered a fractured skull following a collision on the ground with a Ju 52/3m in the East, 'Schorsch' Eder quickly proved his abilities in this tough new form of warfare in the West when he shot down a B-17 on 30 December 1942, with another following four days later.

Following the destruction of a Flying Fortress on 28 March 1943, his Bf 109G-4 was hit in the engine and somersaulted upon landing, as a result of which Eder was seriously injured again. He recovered to fly and fight once more, and by 14 July 1943 Eder had claimed eight Flying Fortresses. On that day, during Eighth Air Force raids on German airfields in France, he shot down two more during the early morning. The last of his B-17 claims while with JG 2, on 30 July 1943, was classified as a *'Herrauschuss'* (HSS) – the 'cutting out' or shooting away of a bomber from its combat formation, thus rendering it damaged and vulnerable to attack. On 5 November Eder had to take to his parachute following combat.

In March 1944, after leading 5./JG 2, Eder was transferred to 6./JG 1, his victory score standing at 33, including 11 B-17s. His record for 'invincibility' held when, firstly, he was forced to bail out of his Fw 190 after being attacked by a P-47 over Göttingen on 19 April, and then when he had to make an emergency landing at Vechta on the morning of 8 May, having shot down a B-24 southwest of Verden. By mid-May 1944 Eder had been appointed *Kommandeur* of II./JG 1, having achieved 43 victories. He

Oberleutnant Georg-Peter Eder (right) with his wingman upon returning from a sortie in which he shot down a *Viermot*. A veteran of the Eastern Front, he became one of the Luftwaffe's earliest specialists against American *Viermots*, and would go on to accumulate 36 four-engined victories. This tally made Eder the highest-scoring German pilot in such operations, with the last of his successes being scored while flying the Me 262

remained in this post until 11 August, when he assumed command of 6./JG 26, before being appointed *Gruppenkommandeur* of II./JG 26 on 4 September when its previous CO, Emil Lang, was killed in action. Days later however, Eder was transferred to oversee the build-up of the first Me 262 jet fighter trials unit, *Erprobungskommando* 262. By then he had shot down 21 four-engined bombers – 16 B-17s (two HSS) and five B-24s. Although Eder's days flying conventional fighters were now at an end, his culling of heavy bombers was far from over.

Then there was Hugo Frey, a native of the Neckar region of Württemberg. Frey had flown with 1.(J)/LG 2 in the Polish campaign in 1939, where he had scored his first victory on 4 September. Aside from the claiming of a Potez 63 in France in May 1940, Frey enjoyed no further success until he joined 10./JG 1 and shot down a Boston on 4 September 1942.

However, the following year, leading 2./JG 1, Frey began to notch up an astonishing scoreboard of four-engined bombers, and he became one of the Luftwaffe's earliest and leading proponents in combat against them. His first such success was a B-17 shot down in clear blue skies on 27 January 1943 – the day the USAAF first launched a mission against a target on German soil when it attacked the ports of Wilhelmshaven and Emden with 55 bombers. Any joy at his success was dissipated, however, by the draining shock of engaging in head-on combat against such monstrous aircraft, as well as the losses incurred in such missions. Although eight of his fellow pilots in JG 1 lodged claims for *Viermots* that day, the USAAF reported the loss of only three B-17s. The *Geschwader* lost eight pilots – a grim portent of things to come.

Throughout the rest of 1943 Frey, who had been appointed *Staffelkapitän* of 7./JG 11 on 1 April that year, accounted for a further twelve B-17s and five B-24s and one unidentified four-engined aircraft, including two B-17s downed on 26 November 1943 plus a P-47 escort fighter. But his zenith was to be reached on 6 March 1944 when the Eighth Air Force attacked Berlin for the first time (see Chapter Two).

During the mid-afternoon, as the American force made its way west back to England, Frey, leading one of two pairs of Fw 190s of III./JG 11, shot down no fewer than four B-17s at close range (all witnessed by his wingman). These aircraft, probably from B Formation of the 45th Combat Wing (CW), were downed in the space of ten minutes over Assen-Alkmaar. Moments later the leader of the other pair of Focke-Wulfs, Hauptmann Anton Hackl, heard Frey cry over the R/T 'I've been hit!' These were the last words heard from the ace, who had almost certainly been hit by defensive fire from a fifth bomber that he had targeted flying with the Low Box of the 45th CW. Several gunners from B-17s in this formation reported downing a persistent Fw 190 near Coevorden, in Holland, close to the German border. Frey perished in the subsequent crash near Sleen, 30 kilometres west of Meppen.

Oberleutnant Hugo Frey was credited with 32 victories, of which 25 are known to have been four-engined bombers. Despite his relatively short time spent on operations against the 'heavies', this tally places Frey in the top-ten highest-scoring recorded *Viermot Experten*. Also, despite these accomplishments, the award of the Knight's Cross was made only posthumously on 4 May 1944, when he was promoted to hauptmann.

A smiling Oberleutnant Hugo Frey, *Staffelkapitän* of 7./JG 11, jumps from the cockpit of his Fw 190 following a sortie over Germany in the autumn of 1943. Frey was one of the Luftwaffe's highest-scoring 'bomber-killers' with 25 *Viermots* to his credit. He was killed by defensive fire from a B-17 while in action over Berlin on 6 March 1944. He had shot down four Flying Fortresses minutes earlier

Oberstleutnant Walter Oesau, one of the Luftwaffe's most tenacious unit commanders and Egon Mayer's predecessor as *Kommodore* of JG 2 from July 1941 to June 1943. 'Gulle' Oesau was the third serviceman to be awarded the Swords to the Knight's Cross and the third German pilot to secure 100 victories. He would account for 14 *Viermots* by the time of his death following combat with an American bomber formation and its escort in May 1944

Finally, there is one other outstanding figure among the early '*Viermot* killers'. On 20 December 1942, two B-17s of the 1st Bombardment Wing had fallen over France to the guns of veteran fighter pilot Major Walter Oesau during a mission against the airfield at Romilly-sur-Seine. As *Geschwaderkommodore* of JG 2, Oesau had enjoyed an illustrious career from his service with the *Legion Condor* during the Spanish Civil War, then as *Kommandeur* of III./JG 3 on the Eastern Front at the time of Operation *Barbarossa*, to being only the third fighter pilot to claim 100 victories, which he achieved on 26 October 1941. He had been awarded the Oak Leaves to the Knight's Cross on 6 February 1941 and was only the third man to be awarded the Swords in July 1941 for his 80th victory. The second of the B-17s shot down on 20 December 1942 represented Oesau's 112th victory, and his third four-engined kill.

The mission to Romilly on 20 December was costly to VIII BC, with German flak and fighters causing the loss of six out of 60 Flying Fortresses. A seventh aircraft suffered irrepairable damage, while a further 29 B-17s and one B-24 were also shot up to varying degrees. Two crew were killed and 58 reported missing, with 12 wounded. This represented the worst losses suffered by the Eighth Air Force in its bombing campaign so far.

Oesau had actually claimed an RAF Lancaster in daylight over France on 17 April 1942 as his first *Viermot* – a relatively rare feat given Bomber Command's nocturnal bombing policy – during a period when he was, theoretically, 'banned' from flying because his exemplary record deemed him to be too valuable. He got around this by claiming that he had been on a routine 'test flight' when he intercepted the bomber! Oesau's victim had been one of a small force of 12 Lancasters on their way across France to carry out an experimental low-level raid on the MAN diesel engine factory at Augsburg, in Bavaria. Oesau had claimed he had shot the British bomber down in a case of spirited self-defence as the aircraft had flown close to his *Geschwader's* airfield at Beaumont-le-Roger. It was his 110th victory. Another B-17 followed on 4 February 1943 to bring his score of *Viermots* to four by the end of that year. This would be his last victory claim until early the following year, Oesau being sent to occupy a number of fighter staff positions, including the role of *Jagdfliegerführer* (Fighter Leader) in Brittany.

For all his accomplishments, he failed to impress British Air Intelligence officers who, in a summary of early 1943 recorded that Oesau 'is said to have a palatial HQ at Beaumont-le-Roger, where he lives in great style, wears extravagant clothes, has three aircraft for his personal use (all of them marked with the Oak Leaves) and where in general an incredible degree of ceremony is maintained. He appears to be a rather unpleasant character, vain of his looks, position and achievement, a stickler for efficiency and etiquette and yet quite willing to leave the real work of running the *Geschwader* to his subordinates'.

Irrespective of any such flaws to his personality and qualities of leadership, Oesau would confound the Allied intelligence officers in the grim days of February 1944 as the Eighth Air Force mounted its relentless campaign of bombing attacks on the German aircraft manufacturing industry. As we shall see, he would take a heavy toll of *Viermots* in the coming air battles that month.

CHAPTER TWO

CORNERED WOLF

At an air power symposium in the USA in 1968, 176-victory Luftwaffe ace Johannes Steinhoff, told his audience: 'The appearance of the bombers in mass in 1943 was the turning point in the aerial warfare of World War 2. The era of sportsmanlike, chivalrous hunting had ended. The air space over Europe had turned into a battleground with fortresses and trenches – and it was our duty to storm these fortifications and break through'.

Steinhoff's analogy of air warfare in 1943 is perhaps best encapsulated by the events of 17 August. That day – the anniversary of its first raid on northern Europe – VIII BC launched an attack against the ball-bearing industry located around Schweinfurt. At 0645 hrs, the first B-17s took-off from England for a mission which, in terms of size, surpassed anything that had gone before. The attack was carried out by two large formations. The first, comprising 146 B-17s from seven bomb groups, would attack the Messerschmitt works at Regensburg-Prüfening and continue across southern Europe to land at bases in North Africa. The second formation, consisting of 230 aircraft from the 1st Bomb Wing had, as its objective, the ball-bearing works at Schweinfurt.

However, unsettled weather over England hampered take-off and the mission lost its synchronisation. It took more than an hour for the first wave bombers to join up and assemble into combat formation. The fighter escorts joined them over the North Sea. Shortly after 0930 hrs the complete formation crossed the Dutch coast.

JG 26 established contact with the bombers over Antwerp. From this moment, German fighters harried the 'heavies' along their entire route over Europe. From its position up sun and slightly above the loosely dispersed American formation, I./JG 26 pounced in a classic head-on attack and inflicted fatal damage on several B-17s. The *Kapitän* of 1. *Staffel*, Oberleutnant Artur Beese, a veteran of the Channel Front and one of the small number of JG 26 pilots sent to the USSR earlier in 1943, was one of the first to score, knocking down a B-17 near Berendrecht at 1130 hrs for his 16th victory, but his first *Viermot* kill.

Hauptmann Hermann Staiger, *Staffelkapitän* of 12./JG 26 in August 1943, claimed a B-17 shot down west of the village of Pesch, northwest of Aachen, during the afternoon of the 17th of that month. Every one of his five kills the previous month had been Flying Fortresses. With an eventual score of 26 *Viermots*, he was one of the leading anti-bomber pilots

Know your enemy – an NCO pilot from JG 2 leans down to study a table-top model of a B-17 fitted with wire cones to indicate the fields of of fire from the defensive guns

A co-pilot aboard a Flying Fortress heading for Regensburg recorded;

'Near Woensdrecht, I saw the first flak blossom, light and inaccurate. A few minutes later, two Fw 190s appeared at "one o'clock level" and whizzed through the formation ahead of us in a frontal attack, nicking two B-17s in the wings and breaking away beneath us in half-rolls. Smoke immediately trailed from both B-17s, but they held their stations. As the fighters

passed us at a high rate of closure, the guns of our group went into action. The pungent smell of burnt powder filled our cockpit and the B-17 trembled to the recoil of nose and ball-turret guns. I saw pieces fly off the wing of one of the fighters before they passed from view. There was something desperate about the way those two fighters came in fast right out of their climb without any preliminaries.

'I watched two fighters explode not far beneath us, disappearing in sheets of orange flame, B-17s dropping out in various states of distress, from engines on fire to control surfaces shot away, friendly and enemy parachutes floating down. The sight was fantastic – it surpassed fiction.'

Beese would score again, claiming another B-17 in the afternoon over Belgium.

Hauptmann Hermann Staiger, *Staffelkapitän* of 12./JG 26 claimed his sixth heavy bomber shot down. The previous month he had been credited with five. Staiger had formerly led 7./JG 51 in Russia, where he proved his skill in anti-bomber work when he accounted for the destruction of three Tupolev SBs in one day on 22 June 1941, with a further four in one day on the 30th of that month. Staiger was shot down by Soviet flak and wounded on 13 July 1941, but was rewarded with the Knight's Cross three days later.

He joined JG 26 in July 1943 following a period as an instructor, and shot down five B-17s in a matter of days, including two from the 306th BG over Kiel on 29 July. But even this would be surpassed on 24 April 1944 when, leading a combined force of aircraft from III./JG 26 and III./JG 3, he attacked a formation of 141 B-17s from the 1st Bomb Division (BD) heading for Oberpfaffenhofen. Flying a Bf 109 fitted with a 30 mm MK 108 cannon in the nose, he shot down two B-17s in the space of just one minute over Donauwörth. Twenty-five minutes later, he claimed an HSS for two B-17s, before destroying another south of Munich – again all within one minute.

Staiger would end the war having destroyed 26 four-engined bombers, making him one of the Luftwaffe's leading specialists in their destruction. In the final weeks of the conflict he flew Me 262s as a major in command of II./JG 7, having by then achieved a total of 63 victories.

Seven confirmed bombers went down to the guns of III./JG 26 that day, including two credited to Hauptmann Klaus Mietusch, the *Gruppenkommandeur*, and two to Oberfeldwebel Heinz Kemethmüller of 7. *Staffel*. Mietusch accounted for his pair when his *Gruppe* intercepted the bombers over Aachen during the afternoon and attacked them for 30 minutes. His victims fell southeast of Schleiden and Lake Laacher. Mietusch had gained his first victory in May 1940 over Dunkirk after having spent a brief period as a PoW of the French when he was shot down by a Hurricane and force-landed behind French lines.

A true frontline veteran, he subsequently flew with 7./JG 26 over Sicily, Malta, North Africa, Dieppe and the USSR. Mietusch's score stood at 29 victories when he was injured in a crash in the East, the engine of his fighter having failed shortly after take-off. Subsequently, appointed to lead III./JG 26 back in the West in July 1943, Mietusch went on to account for 13 four-engined bombers, his last claim being for a B-17 shot down near Paris on 14 June 1944 for his 66th victory. However, he was shot down and killed by a US fighter on 17 September

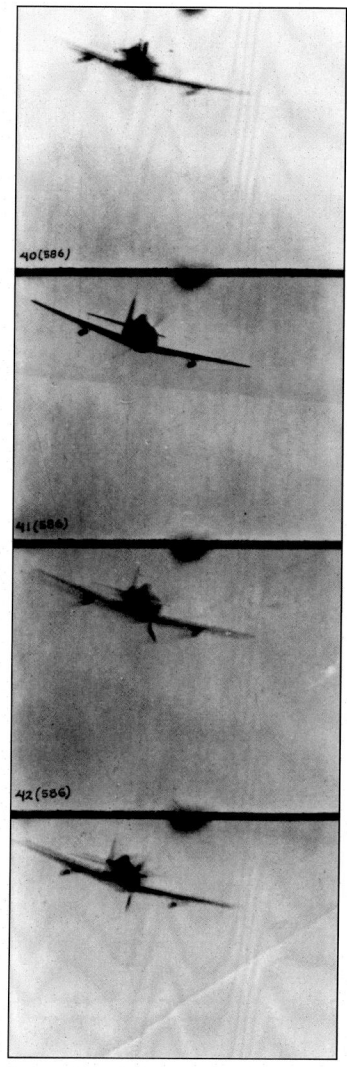

An Fw 190 fitted with underwing 21 cm WGr air-to-air mortars was captured on film as it banked away past a bomber formation during the Eighth Air Force attack on Kassel and Oschersleben on 28 July 1943. More than anything else, the mortars were intended to disrupt and scatter a bomber formation, reducing defensive fire power and increasing the vulnerability of lone bombers

1944. Mietusch's final victory tally was 75, and he was posthumously awarded the Oak Leaves to the Knight's Cross.

Also demonstrating his capabilities in the Schweinfurt raid was the colourful *Kommodore* of JG 26, Oberstleutnant Josef Priller. He had two B-17s to his credit (both scored in June) by the time he downed his third late in the day as the Americans made their return from Schweinfurt. His *Stabsschwarm* and the Fw 190s of Wilhelm-Ferdinand Galland's II./JG 26 met to intercept the Flying Fortresses over the German-Belgian border. Attacking head-on, Priller's B-17 burst into flames and went down north of Liège.

'Pips' Priller's career is well documented, and he is particularly well known for his exceptionally high score against Spitfires, but in context here it is worth noting that of this Knight's Cross-holder's (with Oak Leaves and Swords) 101 victories scored in 1307 combat flights, 11 were known to be *Viermots*. Indeed, his penultimate victory was a B-24 of the 492nd BG shot down west of Dreux in France on 15 June 1944.

In the wake of the 17 August 1943 raid, however, a frustrated Priller was moved to register a complaint to the Staff of the *General der Jagdflieger* about the combat effectiveness of III./JG 1. Its Bf 109s, led by Hauptmann Robert Olejnik, had intercepted the bombers just as the escorting fighters, at the limit of their range, turned back over the Belgian-German border. Priller had noted how JG 1 failed to make a concerted mass attack, preferring to pick on lone 'stragglers' – easier prey. Priller denounced such tactics as those of 'corpse-looters'.

It is fair to say that only two pilots of III./JG 1 scored that day, Olejnik claiming a B-17 for his 41st victory at 1545 hrs and Feldwebel Hans Meissner shooting one down 15 minutes later. Olejnik's account of his kill does, to some extent, verify Priller's point, but equally indicates determination on behalf of the assailant;

'I attacked a bomber to the left of the formation from behind and slightly below. After my third attack, black smoke escaped from its right engine. Little by little, the enemy aircraft became detached from its group, but managed to correct itself 100 m behind, losing 80 m of height in the process – a very uncomfortable position for it. The bomber could no longer count on the protection of its colleagues. It released its bombs, which was the prudent thing to do.

'During my fourth attack the aircraft went out of control. Engulfed in flames, it made three large turns to the left. Seven crewmen bailed out. At 4000 m, the turns became tighter. The right wing broke off, followed by the left wing. The fuselage continued to dive and hit the ground in a wood near Darmstadt. Three men were probably still in the aircraft.'

Claiming two B-17s that day was Leutnant Hans Ehlers of 2./JG 1. He had already downed a B-17 on 6 December 1942 for his 17th victory. The HSS which was credited to him on 17 August represented his 24th kill, with a second B-17 following 17 minutes later. Ehlers had served as groundcrew with the *Legion Condor* in Spain, before joining 2./JG 3, with whom he flew in France. Shot down by a Hurricane and posted missing, he returned to fight over England in the summer of 1940, increasing his score to four. He then saw service in Russia. In the East, Ehlers suffered injuries following a serious ground accident, but returned to the West in September 1941 with his score at 14.

Major Klaus Mietusch, *Gruppenkommandeur* of III./JG 26, claimed two B-17s shot down during the USAAF mission to Schweinfurt on 17 August 1943. Mietusch was one of the 'old hares' of JG 26, having been with the *Geschwader* since 1938. Accredited with 75 victories, including ten four-engined kills, scored in more than 450 missions, Mietusch had been shot down on ten occasions, but he was finally killed when his Bf 109G-6 was attacked by a P-51 over the Dutch-German border on 17 September 1944

Joining JG 1, Ehlers' tally rose steadily. On 8 October 1943, during USAAF raids on Bremen and Vegesack, he shot down a B-17 before colliding with another and being forced to bail out of his Focke-Wulf. Ehlers subsequently received the German Cross in Gold from Reichsmarschall Göring, and on 29 November he again claimed another Flying Fortress. Although wounded by defensive fire from a Boeing bomber on 13 April 1944, Ehlers downed the Flying Fortress over Darmstadt for his 48th victory prior to crash-landing his Fw 190 near Gütersdorf. He returned to service to take command of I./JG 1 and was awarded the Knight's Cross on 9 June 1944. Ehlers was one of six pilots killed during a ground-cover operation for troops in the Dinant-Rochefort area on 27 December, his 18-aircraft formation being attacked by P-51s from the 364th FG. He would be credited with 24 four-engined kills and an overall score of 55.

Pilots of 3./JG 11 wait at cockpit readiness in their Fw 190s at Husum in the late summer of 1943. The nearest machine, 'Yellow 9', carries the *Staffel* emblem of a cartoon pistol imposed on a red heart against a yellow background, with the motto '*Wer zuerst schiesst hat mehr vom Leben*' ('He who shoots first lives longest')

Also scoring a 'double' over B-17s during the Schweinfurt mission was Berliner Hauptmann Erwin Clausen, *Kommandeur* of I./JG 11. He had shot down no fewer than eight Boeings the previous month, his record displaying a pattern of double-claims for B-17s on three occasions – on 26, 27 and 29 July. After successful service in Poland, the Balkans and Russia, Clausen was given the Knight's Cross for 52 victories on 22 May 1942 while flying with 1./JG 77. The month of July 1942 would see Clausen's air combat skills on the Eastern Front reach meteoric levels when he shot down 45 enemy aircraft, claiming four in one day three times, five in one day twice and six in a day on one occasion. Clausen finally achieved 132 victories, and was awarded the Oak Leaves. During his service with JG 11 in the defence of the Reich, he accounted for 12 four-engined bombers destroyed.

Among the pilots seen here about to fly another mission over France is Major Wilhelm-Ferdinand Galland, *Kommandeur* of II./JG 26 (second from left), who was killed in action over Holland during the 17 August 1943 USAAF mission to Schweinfurt when he was shot down by a P-47 while attacking bombers. Galland had been awarded the Knight's Cross and had 55 confirmed victories, including eight *Viermots*

In total, 60 B-17s were shot down and 168 damaged during the Schweinfurt-Regensburg mission. And the destruction inflicted upon the German factories did not compensate for the loss of more than 600 USAAF airmen, as production was interrupted for only a few weeks. The Jagdwaffe was able to celebrate a cautious victory, despite the fact that losses for all participating *Geschwader* amounted to 17 killed and 14 wounded, with 42 fighters destroyed. The losses incurred included that of Major Wilhelm-Ferdinand Galland, Adolf Galland's brother and *Kommandeur* of II./JG

26. A most respected formation leader, he had 55 victories to his credit, including eight 'heavies'.

The war against the bombers ground on – and it grew tougher. Schweinfurt provided the Luftwaffe with valuable lessons in tactical deployment, and on 3 September Galland issued revised directives to every unit engaged in the defence of the Reich;

'The head-on attack is, from now on, to be the exception, and is to be flown in only exceptionally favourable circumstances and by formations especially successful in it. As the standard method of attack, the attack from the rear with a small angle of approach is now ordered.

'From now on, only bombers in formation are to be attacked (without regard to whether they are on the way to the target or on the way out). Only when the entire bomber formation has been broken up or when there is no further possibility of getting to the formation are separated or damaged bombers flying alone to be destroyed.

'Fire will be opened during frontal attacks at a maximum range of 730 metres, and in all attacks at 365 metres. The goal of every attack is one aircraft. Aiming at the centre of a bomber formation or spraying the whole formation with bullets never results in success. Attacks from an angle of approach greater than 30 degrees are ineffective. Combat will be continued even in the strongest flak zones.'

By October 1943 the daylight battle over the Reich had reached its zenith, forcing the Americans to accept that unescorted, deep penetration formations could not adequately protect themselves. Many Luftwaffe pilots were now accumulating noteworthy scores against the *Viermots*. Typical of this period was Oberleutnant Gerhard Sommer of 4./JG 11, whose score of 14 victories included just two that were not four-engined. Sommer had first demonstrated his prowess when he shot down an RAF Wellington in August 1942, but his aforementioned *Viermots* were claimed in the nine months between February and October 1943, including two on one day on 27 August. He was killed in combat with P-47s on 12 May 1944 and awarded the Knight's Cross posthumously.

JG 50 was commanded by the redoubtable Major Hermann Graf, the acclaimed fighter ace from the Eastern Front and holder of the Diamonds to the Knight's Cross. This small *Geschwader* had originally been formed in June 1943 as a high-altitude interceptor unit equipped with just eight Bf 109G-6s. It had been planned to equip JG 50 with the Bf 109G-5, which boasted a pressurised cockpit and GM-1/Nitrous-oxide boost to enhance performance so as to deal with the threat posed by fast British Mosquitoes, but delivery of this variant had been delayed. In the meantime, a greater threat had been presented by the American 'heavies', so the high-altitude 'Mosquito-chasers' were thrown into the battle.

By mid-July, JG 50 had received 12 Bf 109G-5s, and by month-end the unit had shot down its first

As testimony to the resilience of the Flying Fortress, *The Sack* from the 379th BG made it back from the raid to Kassel and Oschersleben on 28 July 1943, despite having been hit by a 21 cm mortar fired by a German fighter, which struck the aircraft below the upper gun turret. The bomber's oxygen cylinders exploded when hit by mortar fragments, blowing a hole in the fuselage

Flying Fortress. On 6 September, during a raid on Stuttgart, Graf accounted for two of four B-17s claimed by his unit that day – these were his 204th and 205th victories. Although the Eighth Air Force lost 45 bombers in total to JG 50 to the end of 1943, the latter's small complement of aircraft was reduced by three and one pilot during this period. Graf, however, would go on to take command of JG 11 in January 1944, and shoot down four more *Viermots* with the unit. Of his 212 victories, just six were four-engined. This statistic is perhaps indicative of the challenging difference between combat in the East and fighting the bombers in the West.

A typical airfield scene from the autumn of 1943 as pilots and groundcrew of II./JG 2 wait at readiness. Bf 109G-6 'White 1' is fitted with underwing MG 151 20 mm cannon

The year 1943 saw Hauptmann Günther Specht's victory tally of 18 consist almost exclusively of B-17s and B-24s – just four of his successes were fighters. The wiry *Kommandeur* of II./JG 11 had lost an eye as a result of defensive fire from an RAF Wellington that he sent crashing into the North Sea in December 1939, but this had affected neither his tenacity nor his gunnery skills. Like Ehlers and Clausen, Specht shot down two B-17s during the cull of the Schweinfurt raid on 17 August 1943. Through 1944, however, he would claim just one B-17 on 22 February, but was awarded the Knight's Cross on 8 April that year. The next month he was appointed *Kommodore* of JG 11, but was posted missing during the infamous Operation *Bodenplatte* on 1 January 1945. Specht was promoted to the rank of oberstleutnant and awarded the Oak Leaves to the Knight's Cross posthumously. He had claimed 34 victories in total.

Former flying instructor Oberleutnant Rudolf Klemm of 7./JG 54 suffered a similar fate to Specht when, on 14 May 1943 during the Eighth Air Force attack on the Kiel shipyards, he shot down his second *Viermot* – a B-24 of the 44th BG that went down just after midday at Rieseby, east of Schleswig. Moments later, in an environment of heavy flak, Klemm's Bf 109G-4 was hit by a shell burst and he was wounded and blinded in one eye. Overcoming this handicap, however, he returned to operations weeks later, and in February 1944 was appointed *Staffelkapitän* of 7./JG 54. To 8 April 1944, Klemm's next seven victories were all heavy bombers, including two B-17s in one day on 20 February and a Flying Fortress (unconfirmed) and a B-24 on 6 March during the attack on Berlin. He survived the war with

The diminutive Hauptmann Günther Specht, *Kommandeur* of II./JG 11, toasts Hauptmann Egon Falkensamer at Jever on 26 May 1943 upon the occasion of his departure as *Staffelkapitän* of 6./JG 11 to an assignment with *Jagdgruppe West*. That year, Specht shot down 14 four-engined bombers despite the loss of one eye

42 victories, including eight confirmed four-engine kills, and was awarded the Knight's Cross on 18 November 1944.

On 10 October 1943 the USAAF struck the marshalling yards at Münster with 206 B-17s, escorted by 216 P-47s. Some 250 buildings were destroyed and a further 3000 damaged, including the railway station and the cathedral. More than 300 inhabitants were killed and 602 injured. In the skies above the city, the Americans encountered vicious and determined aerial opposition – the 100th BG lost 12 of its 14 aircraft. Thirty bombers were downed altogether. Bf 109s from II./JG 3 reached the formation first, and in accordance with Galland's directive, prepared to make an attack from the rear, but they were repelled by the heavy escort. Nevertheless, VIII BC later reported that the attacks mounted by JG 1 and JG 26 against the 3rd BD were 'the most violent and concentrated attack yet made on this Division by enemy aircraft. Attacks, from every clock position, appeared to have a definite method'.

Four days later, 229 of 291 B-17s despatched managed to reach Schweinfurt – a return to attacking aircraft industry targets, which had proved so costly to the Americans in August. It was planned that the bomber force would include 20 B-24s from the 2nd BD, but these – and their escort – were forced to abandon the mission due to bad weather and cloud. Another fighter group had to turn back because of fog, leaving just two groups to escort the B-17s. Over western Germany the weather had cleared, and in cloudless skies I. *Jagdkorps* committed all of its daylight fighter units – a total of 567 aircraft from nine *Jagdgeschwader*, as well as twin-engined *Zerstörer* and some fighter training school aircraft and nightfighters. By the time the 1st BD entered the target area, it had lost 36 bombers, with one group alone losing just under half its strength.

Once the mission was over, the division's losses had increased to 45 machines. One combat wing of 37 aircraft had lost 21 machines. German fighters claimed 149 enemy aircraft destroyed, while losses to the Jagdwaffe during this mission totalled 31 aircraft shot down, 12 written off and 34 damaged – between 3.4 and 4 per cent of available fighter strength in the West.

For the Americans, the battering absorbed by their bombers had been immense. In total, the second Schweinfurt raid had cost 60 B-17s and 600 aircrew. Seventeen more bombers were seriously damaged and a further 121 were damaged but repairable. Despite the catastrophe, Eaker wrote to Arnold the next day with a sense of success, claiming that the Luftwaffe's response was 'pretty much as the last final struggles of a monster in his death throes'. Arnold remained unconvinced, replying, 'The cornered wolf fights hardest'.

The commanding general of the I. *Jagdkorps* recorded that 'the units of the German *Reichsverteidigung* achieved a great defensive success on 14 October 1943'.

Meanwhile, in the Mediterranean in the summer of 1943, German forces were locked in an increasingly marginalised campaign against the Allied air forces operating over Sicily. On 13 May the Axis armies in Tunisia had capitulated, leaving the Allies free to use airfields along the North African coast as a springboard from which to mount air attacks not just on Sicily but on the Italian mainland as well, which was seen as a new frontline. The German fighter force based in the area, comprising elements of JG 3, JG 27, JG 51, JG 53 and JG 77, fought against a large and varied Allied bomber fleet made up of RAF Bostons, Baltimores, Wellingtons, Marauders, Halifaxes and Liberators of the North West African Air Forces, joined by A-20s, B-25s, B-26s, B-17s and B-24s of the US Ninth and Twelfth Air Forces.

Initial tactics deployed against RAF bombers in North Africa were haphazard in nature. Up to 1942, the Luftwaffe had not found it necessary to devise specific tactics against bombers since they were considered to be no great menace in the air. Mainly the *jagdflieger* attempted to use whatever sized force it deployed to a given engagement to firstly attack the fighter escort so as to draw away the cover from the bombers and then to tackle the latter. At first, this basic tactic offered some success. Later, however, as the RAF increased its fighter screens, a greater proportion of the increasingly slender German fighter force was committed to engaging the escort, whilst a small element went for the bombers.

Mass head-on attacks involving at least six aircraft were attempted occasionally, approaching at high speed in a shallow dive, opening fire at 640 metres, closing to 180 metres and aiming at the cockpit. It was hoped to scatter the escorts in the process, but such methods demanded an aircraft and a degree of training and confidence on the part of the pilot not readily found in Africa.

A variation of this method consisted of an approach at height, followed by a steep dive, the fighter coming up under the bomber's tail while opening fire in the climb at the belly of the target aircraft. All such attacks were to be carried out at speed to lessen the time within the range of the bombers' defensive armament.

The Bf 109F/Gs used by the African *Jagdgeschwader* were considered by unit commanders to be 'quite inadequate for the purpose since their manoeuvrability was not sufficient to allow the last-minute violent turns and dives that were an essential part of the tactics'. The Fw 190, better suited for this kind of work, never arrived in sufficient numbers in the theatre. The tipping point came with the arrival in strength of American

A Bf 109G-6/R2 of 12./JG 3 fitted with loaded underwing 21 cm WGr mortar tubes photographed at San Severo, in central Italy, in August 1943. This aircraft is known to have been flown by Leutnant Herbert Kutscha, *Kapitän* of 12./JG 3, and he may have scored some of his six *Viermot* victories in the fighter. It was intended that aircraft so armed should be deployed to break up enemy bomber formations attacking Italian targets from North African bases

heavy bombers in numbers in North Africa at the time when the Germans were in retreat.

Major Johannes Steinhoff had arrived in Tunisia from Russia in early April 1943 as *Kommodore* of JG 77. He recalled;

'It was in April 1943 that I first came in contact with the "four-engine jobs" as we called the B-17s. At that time the battle for North Africa was already lost. On one occasion, after a dogfight with some Spitfires, we were prepared for landing when a glittering armada of bombers of a type we had never seen before, passed above us in the bright midday sun. It was too late to make an attack at that moment, but I would soon have an opportunity to see those giant birds close-up. This occurred after we had regrouped fragments of our *Geschwader* in Sicily and were bringing them back to operational status. The *General der Jagdflieger* had showered us with pamphlets, all concentrating on one subject: "How to attack close-up a formation of bombers".

'The finer points of the doctrine for attacking these bombers had not yet been worked out in the air, but a few principles had nevertheless been established. These were;

'1. Attempt to break up the formation – single aircraft are easy to shoot down.

'2. If you succeed in leading your concentrated fighter force in frontal attack, on collision course, right into the bomber formation, you will be sure to break it up.

'3. Maintain your fighter force in the closest formation possible and do not open fire except at shortest range, but then "fire from all buttonholes" as we used to say.'

Throughout the summer of 1943, the US 5th BW, based in North Africa, used its B-17s to bomb targets in 'softening up' missions on Sicily, Pantelleria, Sardinia and the Italian mainland. In preparation for the invasion of Sicily, which took place on 10 July 1943, the 5th BW launched a series of strikes against the port of Messina, the island's easternmost hub and possibly one of the most heavily defended targets in Europe at that time. On 25 June, in their heaviest raid of the month, 120 B-17s attacked Messina with 300 tons of bombs. In a lecture delivered in 1968, Steinhoff recalled his frustrations with the effort made by *Stab*, I. and II./JG 77;

Know your enemy – under the Mediterranean sun, Sicily-based German fighter pilots receive open air instruction on how to attack a B-24 in 1943. The Liberator has been fitted with wire 'fire cones' to indicate the dispersal of defensive fire, while the fighter model is a Bf 109

'On 25 June our radar stations reported an enemy bomber formation approaching from the Mediterranean about halfway between Sardinia and Sicily, heading for Naples. During the preceding days we had drilled in the new tactics, and I had attempted to prepare our various *Gruppen*, comprising about 120 aircraft, for their first encounter with the four-engined bombers. After we had received take-off orders it was determined that the bombers had not, as expected, attacked Naples port but had instead bombed the ferry traffic between Messina and the Italian mainland. At this point the bombers were already flying in the direction of North Africa, returning to base, and it was almost impossible to make them out on the radar screens because they had gone down to low altitude.

'My formation was able to take off with about 100 aircraft, and it was directed to proceed to the area between Sardinia and Sicily. As we were approaching the area I was advised that the enemy had disappeared from the radar screens and was probably proceeding at almost surface altitude. Visibility was restricted due to strong haze, but just at the moment when I decided to return to base because of fuel shortage, the armada appeared below me.

'The Fortresses were flying in a wide front, only a few metres from the sea, in a formation so huge you could hardly see from one end to the other. It seemed virtually impossible to launch a well-coordinated attack – we had never practiced attacking bombers near the surface. The result was terrible. There was not a single kill, and then the entire German formation went into panic because the majority of the pilots had to be directed back to base by radar. We were also very short of fuel.'

Steinhoff's recollections provide an insight into how it would often 'go wrong' for the defenders, but equally they do not seem consistent with the facts. In fact, Steinhoff is recorded as scoring his 158th victory that day, when he shot down a B-17, while I. *Gruppe* is believed to have accounted for two bombers and II./JG 77 for at least two more, and possibly as many as eight. Such is the 'fog of war'.

As the battle for Italy intensified, so several German pilots performed well in the theatre. For example, in May 1943 Hauptmann Ernst Börngen, *Staffelkapitän* of 5./JG 27, destroyed three bombers over Sicily – a B-25 and two *Viermots* (a B-17 and a B-24). Börngen had been with JG 27 since June 1940, and he flew in operations over England, the Balkans and Russia, before relocating to North Africa in September 1941. He was wounded in air combat on 11 July 1942, having shot down a Spitfire, after which he was forced to land near El Alamein.

Returning to operations, Börngen was made commander of 5./JG 27 and led that *Staffel* during the bitter fighting over southern Italy. On 16 July 1943 he shot down a B-24 east of Bari for his fifth *Viermot*, but his Bf 109G-6 Trop was hit by defensive fire and he was once again forced to land. Following a period of recovery, Börngen served as an instructor with *Jagdgruppe Süd*, before returning to JG 27 in the spring of 1944. He was briefly attached to the *Geschwaderstab* and then III. *Gruppe*, with whom he flew in the *Reichsverteidigung*.

Appointed *Staffelkapitän* of 2./JG 27, Börngen scored his 34th victory – another B-17 (his sixth) – on 23 April 1944 over Willendorf. On 13 May he was appointed to command I./JG 27, and six days later accounted for a pair of Liberators during a mission against 272 B-24s of the 2nd BD that

This photograph of Leutnant Ernst Börngen was taken in December 1941 while he was serving in North Africa with 5./JG 27. Börngen left this theatre with 18 victories to his credit and, from the spring of 1944, went on to serve with distinction in various command positions with JG 27 in the defence of the Reich. On 19 May 1944, he shot down his 16th – and last – *Viermot*, with dramatic results

were targeting Braunschweig. Having shot down the first of his Liberators east of Helmstedt at 1315 hrs, Börngen rammed a second bomber over the same town five minutes later and then took to his parachute. Although he had lost his right arm in the collision, Börngen nursed back to health in the Luftwaffe hospital at Helmstedt. Awarded the Knight's Cross on 27 July, he would see no further operational flying. Börngen's final tally of 38 victories included 16 *Viermots*, seven of them B-24s.

Franz Stigler had also flown with JG 27 (as *Staffelkapitän* of 12. *Staffel*, then with 8./JG 27), and he remembered that 'B-24s suffered from fuel fumes in the fuselage, and that was their weak point. We found that they were easier to shoot down because they burned'. Stigler, who flew 480 combat missions over North Africa, Sicily, Italy and in the defence of the homeland, shot down 28 enemy aircraft flying the Bf 109. He claimed 17 kills over North Africa, followed by five four-engined bombers over Italy and Austria. Stigler was shot down on no fewer than 17 occasions, from which he had bailed out six times. When comparing the Flying Fortress to the Liberator, he recalled;

'The B-17s took a lot of punishment. It was terrifying. I saw them in some cases with their tail fins torn in half, elevators missing, tail gun sections literally shot to pieces, ripped away, but they still flew. We found them a lot harder to bring down than the Liberators. The Liberators sometimes went up in flames right in front of you.

'Attacking bombers became a very mechanical, impersonal kind of warfare – one machine against another. That's why I always tried to count the parachutes. If you saw eight, nine or ten 'chutes come out safely, then you knew it was okay, you felt better about it.

'When you flew through a formation, the B-17s couldn't miss you. If they did something was wrong. I never came back from attacking bombers without a hole somewhere in my aircraft.'

By the time he left the Mediterranean in August 1943, Major Werner Schroer, the *Gruppenkommandeur* of II./JG 27, had claimed the destruction of 13 four-engined bombers – his first, a B-24, going back to 4 November 1942 over Libya. Schroer, like Börngen, was a JG 27 veteran, and he too flew against the B-24s on 16 July 1943, shooting one of them down over Bari – 15 minutes after he had shot one down over Santeramo. His first aerial victory had been over a Hurricane in the desert while flying with 2./JG 27, but he force-landed from that encounter with 48 bullet holes in his Bf 109E. Over Africa, Schroer soon demonstrated an impressive combat record, and was awarded the Knight's Cross on 21 October 1942 for his 49th victory. His ferocity in attacking bombers was demonstrated on 11 February 1943 when he downed a pair of RAF Beauforts in four minutes over Karpathos, followed by two B-24s in one week over Sicily in early May.

This illustrious pilot would go on to claim another 13 *Viermots* in the defence of the Reich, flying as *Kommandeur* of II./JG 27 and III./JG 54, before assuming command of JG 3. With a score of 26 bombers, he would rank as the joint fifth highest-scoring four-engined ace. Schroer ended the war with 114 victories from 197 combat missions, and he was awarded the Swords to the Knight's Cross on 19 April 1945.

Oberleutnant Wilhelm Kientsch served under Schroer as *Staffelkapitän* of 6./JG 27 from June 1943 to January 1944. He had opened up his

While *Gruppenkommandeur* of II./JG 27 from late April 1943 to 3 March 1944, Major Werner Schroer (with his arm in a sling) was credited with the destruction of no fewer than 23 four-engined bombers during the battle over Sicily and later in the defence of the Reich. This photograph shows him some time between November 1944 and February 1945, whilst employed in a senior training capacity with the *Kommandeursschule des Generals der Jagdflieger*

four-engined tally with a B-17 claimed off Trapani on 14 April 1943, but his 'bomber-killing' expertise was demonstrated to the full in May when he shot down four more Boeings in the fighting over Sicily. Kientsch had flown with II./JG 27 since May 1941, and had claimed 16 victories over Africa, 14 of them P-40s. He would shoot down three B-24s in four days between 16-19 July 1943 and, II./JG 27 having later returned to the Reich, claimed a pair of B-17s in one day on 6 September 1943 during an VIII BC attack on aircraft industry targets in the Stuttgart area.

'Willy' Kientsch perished when his Bf 109 struck the ground near Würrisch/Hunsrück, in Germany, after he had become disorientated in cloud during an aerial engagement on 29 January 1944. Of his 53 victories, 20 were over four-engined – an unusually high number for a total of his size. He was posthumously awarded the Oak Leaves to the Knight's Cross on 20 July 1944.

JG 51 numbered among its ranks Hauptmann Karl Rammelt, who had joined the Luftwaffe as a technical officer and been transferred to 4./JG 51 in Russia in May 1942. He scored 15 victories while in the East, including the destruction of five Soviet aircraft in one mission on 5 July 1942. When II./JG 51 was sent to Tunisia in November of that year, Rammelt claimed three Spitfires in 48 hours within days of arriving in the new theatre. His first four-engined kill did not take place until the second Schweinfurt raid on 14 October 1943, however, some five months after he had taken command of his *Gruppe*, and during its brief sojourn in the Reich – he shot down a B-17 over Frankfurt as the USAAF formation made for the target. Rammelt's Messerschmitt was in turn hit by return fire from the bombers, and he was forced to bail out. It was a pyrrhic 30th victory.

Once back in Italy, Rammelt shot down two B-24s south of Rovigo on 28 December during Fifteenth Air Force raids on railway targets in the north of the country. However, the bomber gunners took their toll, blanketing Rammelt's Bf 109G-6 with defensive fire as he made a close-range attack over Padova. Once again the German pilot had to bail out, although this time he suffered serious wounds. Following his return to action, Rammelt was awarded the Knight's Cross on 24 October 1944 for his 41st victory. In an all too familiar pattern, he shot down a B-24 over Hungary on 23 December 1944, took return fire and bailed out again from his Bf 109G-14. Rammelt was so gravely wounded on this occasion that he did not return to combat duty, the B-24 being his 46th, and last, victory. By then he had shot down 11 *Viermots*, most of them Liberators.

Another pilot to make an impact on USAAF bombers in the Mediterranean was Oberleutnant Günther Seeger of JG 53. Having flown initially with 3./JG 2 on the Channel Front in 1941–42, where he notched up 23 victories, 'Hupatz' Seeger joined 6./JG 53 in North Africa in late 1942 and shot down a pair of Bostons on 3 January 1943. His first *Viermot* kill came on 22 March when he claimed a B-17 over Cap Vito, by which time he had transferred to 7. *Staffel*. Seeger had accounted for

Final checks are carried out to the Bf 109G-6 of Leutnant Günther Seeger of 7./JG 53 at a muddy Reggio airfield, in Italy, in October 1943. The aircraft is fitted with a drop tank and underwing MG 151 20 mm cannon, with each gun installation holding 142 rounds. Seeger, seen here in the cockpit, would end the war with eight four-engined victories, five scored in the Mediterranean and three in the West

three more B-17s and a B-24 over Italy by October, at which point he was sent back to Germany with malaria.

In October 1943, Seeger experienced at first hand the destruction and tragedy of the Allied bombing offensive, when his family home in Offenbach was destroyed in a raid. His mother was killed and his father hospitalised. He returned to duty, and in 1944 was appointed *Staffelkapitän* of 4./JG 53, after which he was awarded the Knight's Cross on 26 March. By war's end Seeger's tally stood at 56 victories, of which eight were four-engined bombers.

In the Balkans, December 1943 saw Hauptmann Ernst Düllberg's III./JG 27, equipped with Bf 109s, engaged in defending the Mediterranean, Ionian and Adriatic Seas against RAF Spitfires and Beaufighters. In the final months of the year, however, the unit had also been countering incursions by the US Twelfth and newly-formed Fifteenth Air Forces. On 20 December, for example, Düllberg, who had flown with JG 27 since the Channel campaign in 1940, shot down two B-17s over Eleusis and Megara. His *Gruppe* had first clashed with the heavy bombers of the Twelfth Air Force on 5 October, when B-24s set out to bomb airfields in Greece, Crete and Rhodes. Düllberg had destroyed a Liberator near Lidorikion, while Leutnant Emil Clade and Unteroffizier Rudolf Moycis of 7./JG 27 claimed one each and Oberfeldwebel Fritz Gromotka of 9. *Staffel* also accounted for one.

Altogether Düllberg registered five *Viermots* downed in the Balkans and a further five in the battles over the Reich following III. *Gruppe's* return to Germany in the spring of 1944, bringing his score to ten. He was awarded the Knight's Cross on 27 July 1944 and was appointed *Kommodore* of JG 76 in October of that year. Düllberg spent the final months of the war in Hungary coodinating the operations of JG 76, II./JG 51, II./JG 52 and III./JG 53, before being assigned to conversion to the Me 262. He was credited with 45 victories.

Fritz Gromotka shared Düllberg's propensity for knocking down Liberators in late 1943, scoring a 'double' on 6 December over Eleusis and Milos. He had already displayed his skill at combating light and medium bombers by shooting down two Blenheims in the Balkans on 14 April 1941 and another over Sidi Barrani, in North Africa, on 23 February 1942. A Baltimore, shot down over the Aegean, followed on 4 December 1943. Gromotka served in the Balkans, North Africa and Russia, and like many of his fellow *jagdflieger*, force-landed having run out of fuel, was posted missing on one occasion in the East, crash-landed in the desert and bailed out on five occasions in his service career. Gromotka ended the war having been awarded the Knight's Cross on 29 January 1945 with

Hauptmann Ernst Düllberg stands beside his Bf 109 (possibly a G-2) marked with the chevrons of the *Gruppenkommandeur* of III./JG 27 – the position he held from 11 October 1942 to 30 September 1944, when he assumed command of JG 76. Düllberg would destroy 16 *Viermots* while with JG 27, including several double-victories in one mission

a total of 29 kills, nine being four-engined, including one B-24 and five B-17s (two HSS) over the Reich between March and May 1944.

Meanwhile, the Luftwaffe was beginning to adopt increasingly desperate measures against the bombers in northwest Europe. On 8 November 1943, Galland informed his unit commanders;

'German fighters have been unable to obtain decisive successes in the defence against American four-engine formations. Even the introduction of new weaponry has not appreciably changed the situation. The main reason for this is the failure of formation leaders to lead up whole formations for attack at the closest possible range. Göring has therefore ordered the establishment of a *Sturmstaffel*, whose task will be to break up Allied formations by means of an all-out attack with more heavily-armed fighters in close formation and at the closest range. Such attacks that are undertaken are to be pressed home to the very heart of the Allied formation whatever happens, and without regard to losses until the formation is annihilated.'

This was the brainchild of Major Hans-Günter von Kornatzki, a long-serving officer who had studied gun camera film, combat reports, tactics and weapons intended for close-range work against enemy bombers. Kornatzki advocated adopting radical new tactics involving massed rear attacks against the bomber *Pulks* by tight formations of heavily-armed and armoured Fw 190s. He reasoned that during a rearward attack against a bomber formation, a German fighter was exposed to the defensive fire of more than forty 0.50-in machine-guns, resulting in only the slimmest chance of escaping damage.

Under such circumstances it was unlikely that a lone fighter could bring down a bomber. However, if a complete *Gruppe* could position itself for an attack at close range, the bomber gunners would be forced to disperse their fire, and thus weaken it, allowing individual fighters greater opportunity to close in, avoid damage and shoot a bomber down. The loss of speed and manoeuvrability incurred by the extra armament and armour carried by these *Sturm* aircraft would be countered by the presence of two regular fighter *Gruppen*, which would keep any enemy escorts at bay. Kornatzki also suggested that, if necessary and as a last-ditch resort, in instances where pilots were close enough, and if ammunition had been expended, a bomber could be rammed in order to bring it down. He further proposed that a *Staffel* rather than a *Gruppe* first be established to train up volunteer pilots who would evaluate the new method under operational conditions. *Sturmstaffel* 1 was established in October 1943 and Kornatzki appointed as its commander.

Know your enemy – by mid-1943, German fighter pilots based in the West and the Reich were never allowed to forget their priority target. Here, the formidable frontal view of a B-17 has been painted in scale on the doors of a hangar for range and gunnery purposes. Groundcrew standing below the starboard wing lend scale to the artwork

CHAPTER THREE

'BIG WEEK' AND BERLIN

Between November 1943 and January 1944 volunteers trickled in to *Sturmstaffel* 1's successive bases at Achmer and Dortmund. By the time of the unit's first combat mission on 5 January, there were some 30 pilots on strength, many of them from the training schools eager for action in their unit's heavily armed and armoured Fw 190s, which had been specially adapted for close-quarter work against bomber formations. Operations in January got off to an inauspicious, if not discouraging, start when only four missions were flown throughout the month and just four *Viermots* were shot down.

The pattern of American bombing throughout January was dictated to a great extent by the prevailing overcast weather over northwest Europe, which necessitated pathfinder-led missions against German ports and industrial areas. The only major visual operation occurred on 11 January when the weather was expected to be fine. It was, however, to prove fickle, but the American bomber force of 663 aircraft pushed on in deteriorating conditions to hit several aviation and industrial targets in the heart of the Reich (Oschersleben, Halberstadt, Braunschweig and Osnabrück) on a mission that was to mark the commencement of Operation *Pointblank* – the strategic air offensive against Germany that was designed to bring about 'the progressive destruction and dislocation of the German military and economic system'.

The Luftwaffe was to put up the fiercest opposition since the last Schweinfurt raid, although German fighters would fly only 239 sorties. However, the day saw the first *Viermot* to fall to the guns of *Sturmstaffel* 1 when it mounted a rear attack against a *'Pulk'* (a group or herd) of Flying Fortresses and Oberleutnant Othmar Zehart claimed a kill.

By the end of the mission the USAAF had lost 60 bombers – almost 11 per cent of the total force – with one formation losing 19 per cent of its strength to enemy action. I. *Jagdkorps* reported 21 aircraft lost and a further 19 with more than 60 per cent damaged.

Othmar Zehart, an Austrian, was one of the few pilots believed to have signed an oath to the effect that if a bomber could not be shot down with ammunition he would resort to ramming. Oberleutnant Richard Franz of *Sturmstaffel* 1 recalled;

'At that time we were the only unit which attacked the *Viermots* from the rear, and all the other pilots who flew in the *Reichsverteidigung* thought we were a little crazy. They all preferred to attack head-on, with the advantages and disadvantages that came with it. The *Sturmstaffel* pilots, on the other hand, voluntarily bound themselves to bring down one bomber per engagement, either with their weapons or by ramming. I never had to ram, thank God.'

Two B-24s and another B-17 would be claimed on the 30th, the latter by one of the more experienced and senior officers of the unit, another

The pilots of *Sturmstaffel* 1 line up in front of an Fw 190 at Salzwedel on 29 April 1944. Seen first left is Oberleutant Othmar Zehart and third from left is Leutnant Siegfried Müller, then Leutnant Rudolf Metz, Major Hans-Günther von Kornatzki, Leutnant Werner Gerth, Feldwebel Kurt Röhrich, Leutnant Richard Franz, Feldwebel Wolfgang Kosse and Oberfeldwebel Gerhard Marburg. Fourth from right is Unteroffizier Willi Maximowitz and third from right Feldwebel Oscar Boesch

Austrian, Major Erwin Bacsila. A respected officer, he had frontline experience stretching back to the Polish and French campaigns.

In France Oberleutnant Artur Beese, *Staffelkapitän* of 1./JG 26, struck again on the 21st when he shot down two of the five B-24s from the 44thBG credited to his *Staffel* over Poix during a major Eighth Air Force attack against V1 sites. They would be Beese's last victories, for he was killed when he hit the tail of his Fw 190 as he bailed out following combat with P-47s over Melun on 6 February. Of his 22 victories, six were four-engined bombers.

Eight days later, a former member of 1./JG 26, Leutnant Wilhelm Hofmann, serving with 8./JG 26, shot down a B-17 north of Lutrebois when the USAAF despatched 863 B-17s and B-24s to targets in the Frankfurt area, escorted by 632 fighters. It was Hofmann's third *Viermot* kill that month. He had been with JG 26 since June 1942, and shot down his first victim, a Spitfire, exactly four months later. Hofmann was hospitalised for four months following a crash-landing after his Fw 190 had suffered engine failure on 9 December, but on 31 March 1943 he journeyed to the East where, on 14 May, he downed a LaGG-3.

Returning to the West, Hofmann was given command of 8./JG 26 in February 1944. Following the Allied invasion of June, he demonstrated a formidable combat proficiency, claiming 11 US fighters in the month following the landings, including six Thunderbolts. On 26 March 1945, by which time he was wearing an eye-patch due to a gunnery accident on the ground, it is believed Hofmann was accidentally shot down by his wingman during an engagement with RAF Tempests near Hasselünne. He bailed out but his parachute failed to deploy. Hofmann recorded 44 victories and was a recipient of the Knight's Cross. He had accounted for six *Viermots* destroyed.

In February 1944, prompted by Gen 'Hap' Arnold's directive the previous month to 'Destroy the enemy air force wherever you find them

– in the air, on the ground and in the factories', the Eighth Air Force launched Operation *Argument*, better known as 'Big Week'. This took the form of an intensive bombing campaign against fighter production plants in Germany, commencing on the 20th against the factories at Leipzig-Mockau, Halberstadt and Regensburg.

The offensive was intended to do two things – destroy German aircraft on the ground, and the means of replacing them, and force the Luftwaffe into the air to defend vital installations against aerial attacks. In all, 1000 aircraft were committed to the operation, together with fighter protection from all available fighter groups in both the Eighth and Ninth Air Forces. It was to be the largest force ever assembled in the history of American strategic air power. In comparison, between them, I. and II. *Jagdkorps* could muster approximately 750 serviceable aircraft.

Nevertheless, this imbalance in numbers did not prevent the Luftwaffe from showing its teeth intermittently during 'Big Week'. The first raids mounted against objectives in the Braunschweig and Leipzig areas saw 'unaggressive' and 'remarkably weak' reaction from the defenders, but the later raids provoked an angry response.

At 1516 hrs on 20 February, during the opening raid of the *Argument* offensive, the newly appointed commander of III./JG 2, Hauptmann Herbert Huppertz, shot down a B-17 northwest of Mons, in Belgium. He would claim a B-24 two days later and two B-17s in March.

Huppertz had joined JG 2 from his command of 9./JG 5. Before that he had been a long-serving member of III./JG 51, with whom he had been awarded the Knight's Cross on the occasion of his 34th victory and in recognition of a string of aerial successes claimed on the Russian Front, including the destruction of multiple twin-engined DB-3 bombers in one day on three occasions. Huppertz served briefly in Norway in early 1942 as *Staffelkapitän* of 12./JG 1, and claimed a Spitfire shot down during Operation *Donnerkeil* (the famous 'Channel Dash').

He was credited with his first *Viermot* – a B-17 – on 4 July 1943, but it would be four months until his second such kill. In December 1943, while with 11./JG 2, all four of his victories were American heavy bombers, including two B-17s in one day on the 30th during a raid on Ludwigshafen and a B-24 shot down on the last day of the year. In 1944, Huppertz would go on to claim another eight four-engined bombers destroyed. On the first day of the Allied landings in France – 6 June 1944 – he recorded a remarkable five victories over Allied fighters between midday and 2100 hrs, but two days later his Fw 190 was shot down and he was killed during an action with American fighters near Caen. Herbert Huppertz was posthumously awarded the Oak Leaves to his Knight's Cross and promoted to major. He had 78 victories to his name, 17 of them four-engined bombers.

On 22 February, in the first successful coordinated attack, 1396 bombers from the Eighth and Fifteenth Air Forces, with 965 escort fighters, attacked targets across Germany simultaneously. The operations of the three bomb divisions from the Eighth, however, all of which were attacking airfield targets, were hampered badly by cloud during assembly over England as well as around many of the primary targets. The entire 3rd BD of 333 B-17s was recalled, having travelled 100 miles into enemy airspace, while 100 B-24s of the 2nd BD turned around as well. In all,

544 of the 799 bombers were recalled or forced to abort. According to the Eighth Air Force's post-mission narrative;

'1st BD formations became quite badly scattered, making it impossible for fighters to cover all boxes adequately. Leaving Germany far north of their brief route, these wings were severely attacked by as many as 80 enemy aircraft in the vicinity of Münster and for 50 miles northwest to the Dutch border. The majority of opposing fighters were Fw 190s and Me 109s maintaining ceaseless attacks, coming in at B-17 formations from the nose abreast and following each other through formations again and again.'

Waiting for the bombers as they crossed the Dutch-German border shortly before 1300 hrs was II./JG 26. Leading the Fw 190s of 5. *Staffel* was veteran *jagdflieger* Oberfeldwebel Adolf Glunz, who had shot down a B-17 just 24 hours earlier over Holland. This day, however, would mark a rare personal accomplishment for Glunz. The bomber stream had already been attacked by I./JG 26 and II./JG 1 over the coastal area, leaving the escort scattered and much of the formation vulnerable. At 1250 hrs II. *Gruppe* struck, with Glunz shooting down a B-17, probably from the 91st or 384th BGs, which went down west of Dorsten. The Focke-Wulfs made repeated passes and Glunz claimed an HSS five minutes later, followed by another northeast of Wesel at 1310 hrs, this being his 56th victory of the war.

During the afternoon, as the bombers made for home, Glunz was in the air again from his Dutch base, harrying them with his *Gruppe*. He downed a P-47 escort at 1530 hrs and two more B-17s ten minutes later. Glunz had therefore claimed five Flying Fortresses on this day.

He had commenced his Luftwaffe career with 4./JG 52 on the Channel Front in 1941 and then moved with the *Staffel* to Russia, from where he returned with three aerial victories and credit for the destruction of two enemy tanks. Glunz joined 4./JG 26 in early July 1941, and from 27 August of that year to 14 March 1943, his 23 victories were all Spitfires. He received the Knight's Cross on 29 August 1943 – the only NCO in JG 26 to wear the decoration. Glunz was appointed *Staffelkapitän* of 5./JG 26 on 15 January 1944 and ended the war with 71 victories to his name, 19 of them *Viermots*. He was never shot down or wounded in combat, and from March 1945 he flew the Me 262.

Also successful that day was Oberst Walter Oesau, now commanding JG 1, when he shot down a B-17 during the bombers' approach and another on their exit for his 120th and 121st victories. By the end of February Oesau had claimed six heavy bombers during the course of the month. However, he would be shot down and killed by P-38s on 11 May 1944 as he mounted an attack with his *Stabsschwarm* against *Viermots* bombing marshalling yards in France, Belgium and Luxembourg. His Bf 109 crashed in countryside a few kilometres from St Vith and his body was found close by. Of Oesau's final score of 127 kills, 14 were *Viermots*.

Following its mission to Gotha on 24 February, the 2nd BD reported its B-24 Liberators as 'being attacked almost the entire period over Germany'. It seemed that the Jagdwaffe fighters had gained a new confidence, the Fw 190s of JG 1 and JG 26 'pressing home vicious nose attacks', whilst elsewhere 'some groups were forced far off course, and these formations, and especially stragglers, were attacked unceasingly'.

Oberfeldwebel Adolf Glunz, *Staffelkapitän* of 5./JG 26 and one of the most successful German fighter pilots in the West, hoists himself from the cockpit of his Fw 190A-7 at Cambrai-Epinoy on 22 February 1944. Glunz had just led 5. *Staffel* against an American bomber raid on factories in central Germany. During his unit's attack, he shot down three B-17s and claimed *Herrausschüsse* against two others, as well as downing a P-47 – this proved to be his most successful day as a fighter pilot. Glunz would end the war with 19 four-engined kills to his name

This photograph of Feldwebel Franz Steiner was taken during his time with I./JG 11 in 1944, the pilot performing Reich defence duties over Germany. Steiner was an accomplished fighter pilot who was credited with the destruction of nine four-engined bombers. In early 1945 he was selected by Adolf Galland to join JV 44, with whom he flew the Me 262

That day, the 2nd BD alone lost 33 four-engined bombers, two falling to Feldwebel Franz Steiner of 2./JG 11.

Described as 'a passionate flier', Steiner had flown with JG 27 from the summer of 1940, serving in the Balkans and North Africa. Posted back to Europe in early 1942, he joined 8./JG 1 and was almost immediately moved to Trondheim, in Norway, as part of *Kommando* 'Losigkeit', a special unit formed from pilots of JG 1 intended to offer air protection to vessels of the Kriegsmarine seeking shelter on the Norwegian coast and in the fjords following the 'Channel Dash' out of France. Steiner continued his duties with JG 1 until the summer of 1944, when he spent a brief spell as a fighter instructor with an *Ergänzungsgruppe* in Märkisch-Friedland, before joining 2./JG 11 to fly Fw 190s over the homeland. He subsequently claimed seven B-17s, three B-24s, a P-38 and a B-26 shot down.

The Fifteenth Air Force 'twisted the knife' into the German defences on 24 February, however, when it launched a simultaneous raid on aircraft components factories at Steyr, in Austria. Mortar-equipped fighters from JG 3, JG 27 and ZG 1 attacked B-17s of the 2nd BG, shooting down a 'box' of ten bombers. III./JG 3 did particularly well, claiming six bombers and three HSS.

As to the effects of 'Big Week', on 23 February, during a conference on aircraft production in Berlin, Generalfeldmarschall Erhard Milch confessed;

'The effect on our day fighter production has been very severe and we are faced with great difficulties. If you go into a fighter plant – I have seen Erla-Leipzig and Oschersleben – there is nothing to be seen but bent wires, like a bombed block of flats here in Berlin. Outside there are bomb craters eight to nine metres deep and 14-16 metres across. But the struggle is not hopeless, it can be managed. We should reach a monthly output of 2000 fighters by the end of February.'

I. *Jagdkorps* generated 2861 sorties in February, and losses in its operational area at month-end stood at 299 aircraft, or 10.3 per cent of the total number of aircraft committed. The death toll for February was devastating, and included yet more valued *experten*. Oberstleutnant Egon Mayer, *Kommodore* of JG 2 and the architect of the classic head-on attack, fell prey to American fighters. His loss was especially hard to bear, since he had become one of the highest scorers against the bombers, with 25 *Viermots* to his credit.

Following the attacks on the aircraft manufacturing centres, the Americans next concentrated their efforts on Berlin. The 'hub' of Germany's war effort, the city was both home to the headquarters of the armed services and a major rail centre. The first strike was mounted on 4 March when 500 'heavies', escorted by 770 fighters, headed for the capital. The concept behind the 'Big-B' missions was not solely to bomb

Bf 109Gs of Major Walther Dahl's III./JG 3 undergo engine maintenance at Leipheim in March 1944. The aircraft in the foreground is 'Black 9', and it features a typical spinner spiral and the white fuselage band of the *Geschwader*, as well as the black vertical bar of III. *Gruppe*

major industrial targets, nor even to dent civilian morale, but rather to coax the Jagdwaffe into the air in order to inflict further losses. The Eighth Air Force's trump card was the dreaded Merlin-engined P-51. Equipped with underwing drop tanks, the Mustang could now escort bombers all the way to their targets deep in the heartland of Germany.

Despite this new, but not unexpected, menace, German response to this first, crucial raid was light, and the American losses incurred were more as a result of poor conditions rather than the sporadic reaction by Luftwaffe fighters. Luckily for the city, adverse weather prevented all but 30 aircraft from reaching their primary target, inflicting little damage. Of this force, five aircraft were shot down.

Two days later, however, the story was different. On 6 March, the Americans despatched 730 bombers, with an escort of 796 fighters, from the Eighth and Fifteenth Air Forces to bomb the capital. The Luftwaffe had been expecting the raid and had prepared itself by practising the assembly of large formations of fighters – so-called *Gefechtsverbände* – several days before in an attempt to meet mass with mass. So it was that on this day no fewer than 19 *Jagdgruppen*, three *Zerstörergruppen* and four *Nachtjagdgruppen*, together with a handful of miscellaneous units, were available to take on the *Viermots*. Bitter fighting waged from the moment the bomber streams crossed the Dutch coast, and it lasted all the way to Berlin and back.

For the seven Fw 190s of *Sturmstaffel* 1 operating as part of a *Gefechtsverband* made up of I., II. and IV./JG 3, JG 302, the *Jasta* 'Erla' works defence flight and some *Zerstörergruppen*, it was to be the most successful day since the unit's formation.

Moving in to attack a formation of 112 B-17s of the 1st and 94th CWs of the 1st BD, the *Staffel* closed in on bombers of the 91st BG from the rear just after 1230 hrs. In the space of one minute Unteroffizier Kurt Röhrich scored his third victory, while Unteroffizier Willi Maximowitz claimed an HSS and Leutnant Gerhard Dost downed his first bomber.

Three minutes later, Feldwebel Hermann Wahlfeld, who had shot down two bombers 48 hours earlier, added to his personal score and recorded his third victory. Oberleutnant Othmar Zehart followed at 1255 hrs when he scored his second victory. One Fw 190 collided with a B-17G.

In all, by the time the *Gefechtsverband* broke off its attack, having expended both fuel and ammunition, eight B-17s had been shot down and three more destroyed in collisions. Four P-51 escorts also went down in the Berlin area.

Elsewhere, Channel and Eastern Fronts veteran Leutnant Eugen-Ludwig Zweigart of 7./JG 54 managed to send down three B-17s in engagements during the morning and afternoon. Except for a spell as an instructor in early 1943, Zweigart flew for his entire service career with III./JG 54, and had been awarded the Knight's Cross on 22 January 1943 on the occasion of his 54th victory. Most of his success had been in Russia where, in 1942, he regularly scored multiple kills in one day. Returning with his *Staffel* to the Reich in May 1943, Zweigart went on to down 14 aircraft, only three of which were not *Viermots*. However, his Fw 190 was shot at by Allied fighters over Normandy on 8 June 1944 and he was forced to bail out. He was then apparently shot and killed while descending in his parachute. Zweigart is credited with 69 victories.

Flying into the very centre of the US combat 'boxes' on 6 March, Leutnant Karl Willius, *Kapitän* of 2./JG 26, claimed a B-17 north of Koblenz during the afternoon as the bombers returned to England. 'Charly' Willius had claimed a Spitfire over England for his first victory while flying with 8./JG 51, with whom he remained until July 1941, having scored seven victories while on his first tour of duty in Russia. In a portent of things to come, all these victories were bombers. As an unteroffizier, Willius was assigned to 3./JG 26, and between 8 December 1941 and 12 December 1942 he shot down 11 Spitfires. Awarded the German Cross in Gold on 15 October 1942, he returned to Russia with his *Staffel* and claimed four victories in one day on 13 May 1943.

Willius' subsequent service in the West with 2./JG 26 saw him credited with the destruction of 11 *Viermots*. On 8 April 1944 he made a head-on attack in his Fw 190A-8 against B-24s of the 2nd BD sent to attack aero industry and airfield targets in central Germany, Willius downing one in flames. As the stricken Liberator fell away from its formation, the German ace flew past the bomber and started to climb back into the sun to regroup with his *Staffel*. As he did so, however, he was bounced by P-47s, shot down and killed. Willius' fighter was seen to spin into the ground and explode. By the time of his death he had exactly 50 kills to his name, and was awarded the Knight's Cross posthumously.

However, for the Germans, the price of their 'success' on 6 March was high – 87 single- or twin-engined fighters were lost or damaged. Thirty-six pilots were killed and another 27 wounded.

On the American side, 53 B-17s and 16 B-24s failed to return, 293 B-17s and 54 B-24s were damaged and five B-17s and one B-24 were written off. Seventeen crew were killed, 31 wounded and 686 were listed as missing. It was the highest loss rate for a mission to date. And yet, there was to be no let-up. On 8 March, 320 B-17s and 150 B-24s attacked the VKF ball-bearing plant at Erkner. In addition, targets of opportunity were bombed in the German capital. As an indication of the dramatic odds now facing the Luftwaffe defence, a record 891 USAAF fighters provided escort.

JG 26 was again in action shortly after midday as part of a *Gefechtsverband* with JG 1 and JG 11. The German fighters performed an in-trail attack against the B-17s of the 45th CW over the Steinhuder Meer, west of Hannover. Oberleutnant Walter Matoni was leading the Fw 190s of 5./JG 26 into battle, and he shot down a Boeing bomber over the Mittelandkanal at 1330 hrs, followed by a second ten minutes later near Nienburg for his 15th and 16th victories. The USAAF later recorded;

'3rd BD reported enemy aircraft, mostly single-engined. On the route to Berlin, enemy aircraft were first encountered by this division near Nienburg, and they remained with the formation to the target area. Attacks were directed against lead CW, the 45th, which lost 17 aircraft.'

Major Walter Matoni accounted for 14 *Viermots* shot down during a career that saw him fly more than 400 operational missions. He is seen here during the final months of the war, having received the Knight's Cross for around 30 victories. Matoni was commanding II./JG 2 at this time

Matoni's first victory had been a Hurricane over southern England on 30 September 1940 while flying with 9./JG 27, but as a result of severe wounds, he had spent time in 1942–43 as an instructor with *Jagdgruppe West*. However, he was no stranger to tackling bombers. Matoni had claimed his first *Viermot* during the final stages of the Schweinfurt raid on 27 August 1943 with 6./JG 26. Of the 11 victories he scored between 30 December 1943 and 13 April 1944, just one was a Spitfire. The rest were *Viermots* – six B-17s (3 HSS) and four B-24s (2 HSS). Walter Matoni survived the war with the rank of major. He was credited with 34 victories in total and was awarded the Knight's Cross on 2 January 1945.

At the same time Matoni claimed his first B-17 on 8 March, further to the east, not far from Leitzkau, Knight's Cross-holder Oberleutnant Karl-Heinz Bendert was manouevring his Bf 109 of 5./JG 27 for an attack on Flying Fortresses heading for Erkner. At 1335 hrs his first victim crashed, followed by a second Boeing west of Coburg 35 minutes later. He would claim a B-24 (HSS) a month later on 8 April, taking his final tally of four-engined bombers to ten. Overall, Bendert would claim 55 victories on all fronts, including several multiple P-40, Spitfire and Hurricane kills scored in one day in North Africa between June and August 1942. He also survived the war.

But one of the most prolific bomber-slayers of them all would enter the arena later in the afternoon. Hauptmann Rolf-Günther Hermichen, *Gruppenkommandeur* of I./JG 11, led his Fw 190s into a tough engagement with an outward bomber stream at around 1520 hrs north of Hannover. Within 20 minutes, beginning at 1526 hrs, two B-17s and two B-24s had fallen to the guns of Hermichen, the Flying Fortresses north of Grossburgwedel and the Liberators in the Celle area.

Hermichen had shot down his first enemy aircraft on 10 May 1940 with 6./ZG 1 during the French campaign, and with 9./ZG 76 he took part in the Battle of Britain. On 25 April 1941 9./ZG 76 was redesignated 6./SKG 210 and he was a participant in Operation *Barbarossa*, flying fighter-bomber missions. Hermichen then joined III./JG 26 in November 1941, and in March 1942 was made adjutant to the *Gruppenkommandeur* of III./JG 26, Hauptmann Priller.

After moving to the Eastern Front in January 1943, Hermichen added eight Soviet fighters to his tally. He was appointed temporary

Gruppenkommandeur of III./JG 26 on 15 June 1943, but relinquished command to Klaus Mietusch on 4 July 1943 and returned to 3./JG 26 as *Staffelkapitän*. On 16 October 1943, Hermichen was appointed *Gruppenkommandeur* of I./JG 11, based at Husum. He led this unit successfully until April 1944, after which he took over command of the fighter training unit, II./JG 104.

Hermichen was a true 'bomber-killer', for in addition to his 8 March achievement, he shot down two B-24s in one day on 1 December 1943, four B-24s on 20 February 1944 and three B-17s during the raid on Berlin on 6 March. His final tally of *Viermots* stood at 26. Hermichen was awarded the Knight's Cross on 26 March 1944, followed by the Oak Leaves on 19 February 1945. He survived the war with 64 victories.

Hermichen's fellow *Gruppenkommandeur* in JG 11 was Hauptmann Anton Hackl, commander of III. *Gruppe*. Ten days after the American raid on Erkner, the Eighth Air Force mounted an attack with 678 bombers in clear weather against aircraft industry targets and airfields in the south of Germany. III./JG 11 was one of 20 fighter *Gruppen* deployed to counter the incursion, and it had transferred from the north to Wiesbaden-Erbenheim by early afternoon so as to catch the bombers as they approached their targets. With Hackl leading, the Fw 190s of III./JG 11 made an *Alarmstart* at 1415 hrs and, accompanied by I. *Gruppe*, they intercepted the B-24s of the 14th CW south of Freiburg. The wing was already on the first stage of its return flight, having bombed Friedrichshafen. The Liberators were flying without escort.

Carnage followed. At 1515 hrs, making a rear attack, Hackl shot down a B-24 northeast of Freiburg, and within ten minutes another two had fallen to his guns in the same area for his 137th to 139th victories. Hackl was not alone, however, for 16 pilots from JG 11 made claims against the Liberators during a 15-minute period, including a pair in two minutes to Oberfeldwebel Laskowski of 8. *Staffel*. Many other bombers were damaged in the Focke-Wulfs' attack.

Anton Hackl wore the Oak Leaves to the Knight's Cross, and by 8 March, with 136 victories to his credit (including ten *Viermots*), was one of the Luftwaffe's principal tacticians and a leading 'bomber-killer'. Most of his combat career had been spent with 5./JG 77, and he had scored his first victory with that unit over a Hudson in Norway on 15 June 1940. Moving to Russia, between the opening of *Barbarossa* and 14 January 1943, Hackl accounted for the destruction of 119 aircraft, with many daily multiple claims. He was appointed *Staffelkapitän* of his unit on 23 January 1942 and was awarded the Knight's Cross in recognition of his 51st victory on 25 May 1942, with the Oak Leaves following in August. In July of that year alone Hackl downed no fewer than 37 enemy aircraft.

After a brief spell in North Africa, where he was wounded in action, he was posted to *Stab* III./JG 11 in the defence of the Reich, and weeks

In late October 1943 Rolf-Günther Hermichen, seen here (left) being interviewed for a propaganda radio broadcast, was appointed *Gruppenkommandeur* of I./JG 11 at Husum. He led this unit successfully until April 1944, after which he took over command of the fighter training unit II./JG 104. Hermichen was a true 'bomber-killer', and his tally of *Viermots* eventually stood at 26. He was awarded the Oak Leaves to the Knight's Cross on 19 February 1945 and survived the war

later he was given command of the *Gruppe*. Hackl led III./JG 11 until July 1944, and for the rest of the war he held various command positions, including acting *Kommodore* of JG 11, *Kommodore* of JG 76, commander of II./JG 26 and acting *Kommodore* of JG 300. Hackl flew more than 1000 combat missions, was awarded the Swords to the Knight's Cross and was credited with 192 enemy aircraft destroyed, including no fewer than 34 four-engined bombers, making him the second highest-scoring *Viermot* ace after Georg-Peter Eder.

The 23 March saw *Sturmstaffel* 1 return to the fray with a vengeance when a total of 707 B-17s and B-24s headed for the cities of Braunschweig and Münster and the airfields at Achmer (*Sturmstaffel* 1's original base) and Handorf – all secondary targets and targets of opportunity due to bad weather. The *Sturmstaffel* led by von Kornatzki, together with aircraft from IV./JG 3, took off from Salzwedel and set course for Magdeburg, where it assembled at 1015 hrs with more aircraft from II./JG 3. Once split up into composite battle groups, this force headed west towards Münster.

At 1100 hrs contact was made with the 296 B-17s of the 1st BD, which were flying due west after bombing their target at Münster. Although the Flying Fortresses appeared to be well covered by a heavy escort of P-51s, the German formation overflew the bomber *Pulk* from the left, wheeled ahead and at 1120 hrs, from north of Hamm, launched a massed frontal attack. Within the space of ten minutes *Sturmstaffel* 1 accounted for six B-17s shot down or forced out of formation.

Kornatzki claimed an HSS (his fifth victory), as did Berliner Flieger Wolfgang Kosse. An experienced fighter pilot, Kosse had suffered the ignobility of being demoted from oberleutnant in the summer of 1943 to the lowest rank. He had been relieved of his command of 1./JG 5 in Norway as a result of making an unauthorised flight and damaging an aircraft in the process. Kosse had claimed 11 victories with II./JG 26, the first on 17 May 1940, and later became *Staffelkapitän* of 5./JG 26 on the Channel Front. He was subsequently appointed as the *Staffelkapitän* of 1./JG 5. Perhaps as a means of regaining his reputation and rank, Kosse volunteered for the *Sturmstaffel*, where he claimed six *Viermot* kills. Eventually regaining his rank, he was given command of 13.(*Sturm*)/JG 3 in October 1944, but was posted missing on 24 December 1944. Kosse was credited with at least 28 kills (the last two on the day of his death), of which six were known to have been *Viermots*.

Major Anton Hackl, *Kommodore* of JG 76 (right), assists in rolling out his Fw 190 during the summer of 1944. In addition to his leadership of JG 76, Hackl was an acting *Kommodore* of JG 11, *Kommandeur* of II./JG 26 and acting *Kommodore* of JG 300. He was a recipient of the Swords to the Knight's Cross, and was credited with 192 enemy aircraft destroyed, including 34 *Viermots*, ranking him as the second highest-scoring bomber-killer after Georg-Peter Eder

Also scoring against the bombers on the 23rd was Unteroffizier Gerhard Vivroux when he downed a B-17 between Hamm and Dortmund at 1115 hrs. Vivroux was one of the original cadre of the *Sturmstaffel* joining the unit in November 1943. Assigned to IV./JG 3 in mid-1944, he made a claim with the unit on 12 May 1944 but his Focke-Wulf was hit in the engagement and he was forced to bail out and was seriously wounded. Back at the front by August 1944, his tally reached 11 kills, all but one of which were four-engined. Vivroux died of wounds on 25 October 1944, these having been inflicted by defensive fire from a bomber on 6 October 1944 whilst he was serving with 14./JG 3.

Wolfgang Kosse (second from right) of *Sturmstaffel* 1 describes his shooting-down of a B-17 north of Hamm on 23 March 1944 to one of the *Sturmstaffel*'s senior officers, Major Erwin Bacsila (right). To the left of Kosse is Unteroffizier Kurt Röhrich, who also claimed a B-17 during the mission. Listening to Kosse third from left is Leutnant Rudolf Metz

The attrition meted out in March forced the Eighth Air Force to write off 349 bombers over a period of 23 operationally active days, 13 of which involved all-out effort. 'The total number of bombers hit by or lost to enemy fighters on deep penetrations under visual conditions remains at high levels', the HQ of the Eighth Air Force warned, 'With increased firepower and attacks pressed to close range, the enemy has made his attacks at least twice as effective in loss and damage per attack'.

Yet, for the Luftwaffe, the months of February and March 1944 marked a grim chapter in its history. Pilot losses had been crippling, and were no longer confined to the younger and less experienced, hurriedly trained replacements. The dilemma was now the increasing loss of valuable, experienced and virtually irreplaceable unit leaders. As an example, in the four days from 15-18 March 1944, III./JG 3 flew four missions stretching from Holland to Augsburg and lost five pilots, with six more wounded and another seven forced to either make emergency landings or bail out. Its losses included 108-victory Knight's Cross-holder Hauptmann Emil Bitsch, *Staffelkapitän* of 8. *Staffel*.

Unteroffizier Gerhard Vivroux and Feldwebel Hermann Wahlfeld pose for the camera in front of an Fw 190A-7 at Salzwedel in early 1944. All but one of Vivroux's 11 victories were four-engined bombers. The Focke-Wulf has been fitted with armoured glass panels to the cockpit for defence during close-range attacks on bomber formations

BLOODY APRIL

Throughout April 1944, the American bomber offensive ground on, targeting aircraft production plants in central and southern Germany, while Eighth Air Force fighters and tactical fighters of the Ninth Air Force started strafing airfields. No airspace was safe.

Typical of the units committed to the frontline defence against the USAAF bombers at the beginning of April was II./JG 1 under the command of Major Heinz Bär at Störmede, 11 km southeast of Lippstadt. The *Gruppe* had been formed in January 1942 and had fought its war exclusvely in the defence of Holland and the northwestern approaches to the Reich. Initially equipped with Bf 109s, it had converted to the Fw 190 in mid-1942. Heinz Bär had assumed command upon the death of his predecessor, Hauptmann Hermann Segatz, who had been killed in action during the raid on Berlin on 6 March.

The *Gruppe* had moved its 45 Fw 190s and a single Bf 109 to Störmede from Rheine during the first week of April.

Heinz Bär was one of the Jagdwaffe's most experienced and accomplished pilots. His service career stretched back to 1939, when he scored his first kill in the west. Concluding the Battle of Britain with 17 confirmed victories, he subsequently flew in Russia with JG 51, and within two months had accumulated 60 kills. The award of the Knight's Cross came in July 1941, followed by the Oak Leaves in August. Leaving Russia in 1942, Bär was given command of I./JG 77, with whom he flew over the Mediterranean, claiming another 45 victories (and gaining the Swords to the Knight's Cross) despite contracting a punishing bout of malaria and being stricken by gastric ulcers. Some sources also state that his fighting spirit took a dent.

In the summer of 1943, after a difficult relationship with Johannes Steinhoff, the *Geschwaderkommodore* of JG 77, Bär was transferred to France for apparent 'cowardice before the enemy', where he took command of operational training unit *Jagdgruppe Süd*. One airman commented of Bär, 'Actually, from what one has heard about Bär, he was a "tough" who was avoided as much as possible by the officer corps'.

Ill and exhausted by endless combat, Bär returned to Germany for a period of convalescence, before embarking on a long, hard stint as one

Major Heinz Bär was one of the Luftwaffe's most accomplished *jagdflieger* and unit commanders by war's end, having achieved around 220 aerial victories. His bluntness brought him into conflict with Göring who, later in the war, quietly transferred him away from frontline command and assigned him to lead the Me 262 training and conversion *Gruppe*, III./EJG 2

A pair of Fw 190As of 6./JG 1 in their crude earth revetments at Störmede in April 1944. The aircraft in the foreground bears the winged '1' emblem of *Jagdgeschwader* 1 and the red fuselage identification bands of the *Geschwader*

of the foremost operational commanders in the defence of the Reich. However, once home, his plain speaking on tactical policies did not enamour him to Göring, who saw fit to 'demote' him. Thus, his first posting in Germany was as a 'mere' *Staffelkapitän*. Tenacity and an undeniable combat record, however, meant that it was not long before Bär was once again entrusted with more senior command and appointed *Kommandeur* of II./JG 1. Bär's *Staffelkapitäne* were all experienced men. leading 4. *Staffel* was Oberleutnant Eberhard Burath, while 5./JG 1 was commanded by Oberleutnant Rüdiger Kirchmayr and 6. *Staffel* led by Oberleutnant Georg-Peter Eder (see Chapter One).

On 8 April fog prevented a large part of the 1st BD from taking off to attack its assigned airfield target at Oldenburg. The 3rd BD despatched 255 B-17s to airfields across northwest Germany and the Liberators of the 2nd BD headed for aircraft plants at Braunschweig, as well as Langenhagen airfield and other targets. The whole force was protected by 780 fighters. At 1250 hrs, II./JG 1 was given the *Alarmstart* order and 36 Fw 190s scrambled from Störmede to rendezvous with I. and III. *Gruppen*. Ordered towards Brocken, shortly after 1330 hrs the *Gruppe* sighted a formation of approximately 300 B-17s and B-24s with around 30-40 escorts on its inbound course between Braunschweig and Magdeburg. Twenty minutes later, II./JG 1 made a mass attack on a formation of some 50 Liberators of the 2nd BD from ahead and below.

Heinz Bär scored first, knocking a B-24 down at 1350 hrs for his 198th victory, while Georg-Peter Eder claimed his 34th victory a minute later when he targeted one of two bombers flying to the outer right-hand side of the *Pulk*. He observed hits in the fuselage and starboard wing and the Liberator burst into flames, falling away from its formation and crashing southwest of Salzwedel. Flying alongside Eder at 7000 metres in 6. *Staffel* was Feldwebel Wolfgang Brunner in Fw 190A-7 'Yellow 6'. At 1352 hrs he also selected a bomber to the right of the formation and opened fire with two bursts of his MG 151 20 mm cannon at 600 metres, closing to 200 metres. 'On the second burst', wrote Brunner, 'the Liberator began to burn in the rear half of the fuselage and the wing broke away. The burning fuselage plunged perpendicularly to the ground'. Brunner's victim also came down southwest of Salzwedel. It was his second victory.

In the space of just two minutes, II./JG 1 shot down nine B-24s. A tenth claim, by Unteroffizier Zinkl of 6. *Staffel*, was unconfirmed. Altogther, the 2nd BD lost 30 Liberators to enemy action that day.

Twenty-four hours later, the USAAF targeted aircraft plants and airfields in northeast Germany. More than 400 *Viermots* were effective over the range of targets, escorted by 719 fighters. Eleven fighter *Gruppen* were sent to intercept them, with II./JG 1 in operation as part of a larger *Gefechtsverband* during the

Major Heinz Bär, the *Gruppenkommandeur* of II./JG 1, addresses his pilots at Rheine in March 1944. Pilots who claimed *Viermot* victories in April 1944 included Rüdiger Kirchmayr (far left), Eberhard Burath (second from left), Otto Bach (front row, eighth from left), Leo Schuhmacher (front row, ninth from left) and Kurt Niedereichholz (front row, tenth from left)

morning. Oberleutnant Eder claimed a B-24 (his 35th victory), followed by a P-47, and Feldwebel Heinz Kahl of 6. *Staffel* also accounted for a B-17 and a B-24 for his sixth and seventh victories. However, Zinkl, victor in the previous day's operation, was shot down but bailed out, as did Flieger Georg Blech of 5./JG 1. The *Gruppe* lost Leutnant Meinhard Quack of 4. *Staffel* when he was hit by defensive fire from the bombers and crashed into the Ostsee, while a wounded Unteroffizier Willi Sievers crash-landed at Rheine.

Following the action of the morning, Oberfeldwebel Leo Schuhmacher of *Stab* II./JG 1 and Feldwebel Kurt Niedereichholz of 5. *Staffel* both landed at Rothenburg, along with aircraft of I./JG 11. Here, their Fw 190s were rearmed and fitted with drop tanks. At 1450 hrs these two pilots, with Schuhmacher leading the JG 1 *Rotte* in his Fw 190A-7 'Red 22', took off on an *Alarmstart* with six aircraft from I./JG 11 and headed north for Schleswig-Holstein, where they were vectored to intercept returning bombers of the 1st and 3rd BDs.

Spotting '50-60 B-17Fs' north of Schleswig, the JG 1 pilots lined up to attack the Flying Fortresses to the right of the formation head-on, following in the wake of JG 11. In his Fw 190A-7 'Black 12', Niedereichholz, who had been suffering from a failed R/T, closed in from 500 metres to the 'closest possible range' and opened fire on a bomber with all guns. He scored hits in the cockpit area, a part of which flew away, after which the aircraft went into a steep spiral to the left. At 3500 metres the tail unit and horizontal stabilisers broke away, and Niedereichholz observed three parachutes exit before the burning B-17 smashed into the ground north of Schleswig. It was his 16th victory.

As the Focke-Wulfs flew through the enemy formation Schuhmacher attempted to jettison his drop tank in order to be able to manouevre effectively against the P-47 escorts, but it would not fully disconnect and he had to escape down and away from the formation. As he did so he saw fragments of Niedereichholz's victim fall around him.

On the 11th the Americans launched an all-out assault against centres of aircraft production in eastern Germany. A record-breaking force of 917 B-17s and B-24s was assembled to strike at the Focke-Wulf plants at Poznan and Sorau, the Junkers plants at Bernburg and Halberstadt, aero-engine works at Stettin and Cottbus and various assembly plants at Oschersleben. This enormous armada was protected by more than 800 fighters drawn

Major Heinz Bär visits the wreckage of B-17F *MISS OUACHITA* of the 91st BG, which he shot down on 21 February 1944. He is accompanied by his two usual wingmen, Oberfeldwebel Leo Schuhmacher and Feldwebel Max Sauer (killed on 29 March 1944). Bär insisted on the fact that his wingmen were sufficiently experienced to be able to lead the *Gruppe* themselves in case of his absence

Wearing a prized American flying jacket, Oberfeldwebel Leo Schuhmacher (left) of *Stab* II./JG 1 joins his commanding officer, Heinz Bär (centre), and Feldwebel Max Sauer in examining the top turret of B-17F *MISS OUACHITA*

from 13 groups from the Eighth Air Force and four from the Ninth Air Force's 3rd Division, although with bombers stretched over such a wide range of deep penetration targets, even this escort was barely adequate, especially in poor weather conditions.

In response, I. *Jagdkorps* sent up 432 single- and twin-engined fighters drawn from 1., 2. and 3. *Jagddivision*. Twenty-four Fw 190s of II./JG 1 had been waiting at *Sitzbereitschaft* – cockpit readiness – for eight minutes at Störmede when, at 0958 hrs, *Alarmstart* was ordered. The *Gruppe* flew over Lippspringe to assemble with I. and III./JG 1 over Paderborn, after which the *Geschwader* was to link up with elements of JG 27, but this did not happen. Led by Bär in his Fw 190A-7 'Red 23', the *Gruppe* then passed from 3. to 2. *Jagddivision* and was directed towards a stream of 200+ B-17s and B-24s heading on a northeasterly course. Upon visual contact with the enemy formation north of Braunschweig, II./JG 1 swung to the left and formed up to make a mass head-on attack against a *Pulk* of approximately 15-18 Flying Fortresses.

At 1059 hrs, approaching Fallersleben, and at an altitude of 6000 metres, Bär selected the lowest squadron to the left of the *Pulk* and closed in ahead and slightly below from 400 to 50 metres, opening fire with both MG 151s and MG 131s. His targeted Boeing took hits in the cabin area and fuselage and immediately veered over to port, entering into a sharp spin. The presence of escort fighters prevented Bär from observing the bomber hit the ground, but it would be his 199th victory.

Flying with Bär as his wingman in 'Red 22', Leo Schuhmacher aimed at the same area of the formation and, one minute later, opened fire at the same range with 160 rounds of incendiary and armour-piercing ammunition. 'His' B-17 took hits in both starboard engines and its cockpit, whereupon a stream of white smoke trailed back from beneath the bomber's right wing. Seconds later, as Schuhmacher passed the Boeing he also saw flames. He claimed a B-17 for his 13th kill.

5./JG 1 proved equally deadly. At 1100 hrs in Fw 190A-7 'Black 2', Oberfeldwebel Otto Bach, who had joined JG 1 from 1./JG 2 in 1942 with four victories to his credit, fired at a B-17 at close range and its left wing came away, followed quickly by pieces of the cockpit canopy. Bach saw three men bail out, but the aircraft then plunged into the earth north of Fallersleben. The Boeing was Bach's 13th victory. Flying as his wingman was Flieger Georg Blech in Fw 190A-7 'Black 6', who had been forced to bail out two days before. Blech was now about to issue retribution on the bomber flying alongside Bach's target for his his first aerial victory. Opening fire from 200 metres to close range, Blech scored hits along the left underside section of the fuselage and the inner section of the left wing, both of which began to burn. The B-17 turned over and went down in a steep descent, crashing north of Fallersleben.

At precisely the same moment, at 6000 metres, veteran *jagdflieger* and *Staffelkapitän* of 6./JG 1, Georg-Peter Eder, had closed in to within 100 metres of a B-17 in Fw 190A-7 'Yellow 4'. Opening fire, he raked the bomber with cannon fire from slightly below, sending strikes into its starboard wing as well as along the fuselage. Although the Boeing was seen falling towards the earth by four of Eder's fellow pilots, he was himself attacked by the escorts as he came out of the *Pulk* and had to veer away quickly in an evasive manoeuvre. The bomber came down 10-15 km north of Fallersleben for Eder's 37th victory. Flying as wingman to Eder was Oberfeldwebel Kurt Brodbeck in Fw 190A-7 'Yellow 15', and he also sent a Boeing falling away to port, its fuselage and left wing burning. Although Brodbeck was unable to see the B-17 crash, he was awarded a victory for an enemy aircraft that came down north of Fallersleben. It was Brodbeck's second victory.

After the *Gruppe's* pass through the bombers, due to the strength of the fighter escort it was not possible to reassemble for a second attack, and the subsequent combat broke down into indivdual engagements fought at *Rotte* and *Schwarm*-strength.

By the time II./JG 1 returned to Störmede, it had downed seven bombers in 60 seconds, including an unconfirmed kill to Oberleutant Eberhard Burath. Four pilots were lost to the escorts, but the *Gruppe* also lost seven Fw 190s during a strafing attack on Störmede.

According to the Eighth Air Force, the Luftwaffe performed 'one of its most severe and well coordinated defences, marked by skilful handling of a considerable number of single-engined fighters in the Hannover-Oschersleben area'. Twenty B-17s were lost to fighters out of a total of 52, plus 12 B-24s, whereas I. *Jagdkorps* reported the loss of 36 aircraft. Thirteen German pilots were killed, 17 wounded and a further 24 missing. The 1st BD reported, 'Severe opposition was concentrated against the leading combat wing, which lost 12 aircraft to enemy aircraft or flak. The second fighter attack began at 1102 hrs north of Braunschweig when about 40 enemy aircraft in four-abreast made vicious sweeps through the formation during a gap in fighter support'.

On 13 April, aircraft plants were again the targets for the Eighth Air Force as the offensive switched to southern Germany. This time it was to be the turn of the ball-bearing factories at Schweinfurt, the Messerschmitt plant at Augsburg, the Dornier plant at Oberpfaffenhofen and Lechfeld airfield. Of 626 bombers despatched, 566 were effective over the targets, escorted by nearly 900 fighters.

II./JG 1, already on *Sitzbereitschaft*, was given an *Alarmstart* at 1247 hrs and assembled with the rest of the *Geschwader* at 1000 metres over Paderborn, heading on a southerly course to intercept the incoming bombers. At 1350 hrs visual contact was made with an enemy formation at 6500 metres – elements of the 1st BD – in the Frankfurt area with a strong P-47 escort. Five minutes later, I. and II./JG 1 launched a mass frontal attack on a *Pulk* of approximately 50 B-17s. Once again, Georg-Peter Eder was in the fray in his 'Yellow 4' at 1357 hrs;

'I attacked a Boeing on the right wing of the *Pulk* from the front and below from a range of 600-100 metres. It took hits in the fuselage and in the cabin, veered off course, went straight down 100 metres and then blew apart in the air.'

Leading a *Rotte* from 5. *Staffel* was Unteroffizier Hubert Swoboda.

Oberfeldwebel Otto Bach (centre) of 5./JG 1 with his groundcrew in front of his Fw 190, which bears the winged '1' emblem of JG 1. Bach shot down a B-17 near Fallersleben on 11 April 1944 for his 13th victory

At the same moment Eder shot down his B-17, Swoboda, who was flying Fw 190A-7/R2 'Black 4', opened fire from 300 metres. Closing in on a bomber flying in the second to right position on the right of the *Pulk*, Swoboda recorded that 'the cabin and part of one of the right-hand engines flew away and the Boeing burned, going steeply down'. It was Swoboda's sixth victory. Both Eder's and Swoboda's targets had crashed in an area 20 km southwest of Aschaffenburg. In this attack, II./JG 1 knocked down three *Viermots*, including one that went unconfirmed by Unteroffizier Alfons Schulz of 4. *Staffel*. There were no losses.

Following this operation, aircraft returned to various airfields around Frankfurt and Darmstadt. At Wiesbaden-Erbenheim, fighters from I. and II./JG 1, having been rearmed, were formed into a *Gefechtsverband* and sent up on a second *Alarmstart* at 1505 hrs to engage returning bombers. Contact was made at 1530 hrs south of Heidelberg, but the '200' bombers heading on a northwesterly course were protected by a strong escort. Only one success was possible when, for the second time that day, Swoboda managed to break through at 6500 metres altitude;

'I positioned myself for an attack from the rear and below and fired at the outer right-hand Boeing in the rearmost *Pulk* from a range of 200 metres down to almost ramming range, at which point sections of the left wing and tail assembly flew away. I also saw three of the crew bail out with parachutes. The Boeing went steeply over onto its right wing and down, exploding in flames on the ground. During my exit I received hits, and I was wounded and had to bail out.'

Swoboda's victim crashed near the village of Ittlingen, northeast of Eppingen, while he landed about a kilometre northwest of Eppingen. Taken to hospital in the town by a Luftwaffe officer, he was treated for a head wound. Swoboda's aircraft had crashed 200 metres from the headquarters of a Luftwaffe ground unit.

The Eighth AF recorded, 'Of the three bomb divisions, the 1st met the heaviest air opposition. At around 1400 hrs, another series of attacks was launched ten minutes before Schweinfurt, and these continued for about half an hour. The lead combat wing, which sustained the heaviest losses, was first attacked at about 1350 hrs near Klingenberg. Eight B-17s of the high group were shot down in about three minutes'.

During the afternoon of the 22nd, 638 bombers from all three bomb divisions were despatched against the marshalling yards at Hamm, while smaller forces attacked Bonn, Koblenz and Soest. As part of the German response, the *Gruppen* of JG 1 were given an *Alarmstart* just after 1745 hrs, and on this occasion set off to tackle the bombers individually. I. and II./JG 1 made contact with the B-17s of the 3rd BD north of Hamm at 1850 hrs. I./JG 1 mounted a close frontal attack and shot down four *Viermots*, as well as claiming a HSS. From II. *Gruppe*, it was Flieger Blech in Fw 190A-8 'Black 10' who opened the account when he claimed two B-17s at 700 metres at 1910 hrs;

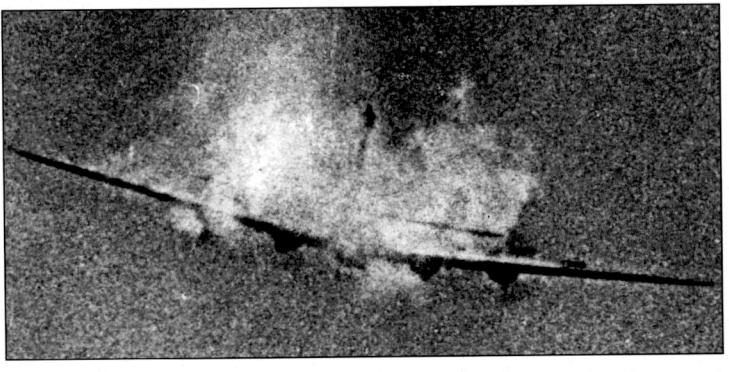

Smoke clouds around a B-17 as it takes hits from a Luftwaffe fighter during a rear-mounted attack

'I attacked, with my *Rotte*, the second Boeing *Pulk* from behind and from the left, firing at the left outer wing of a Boeing at the closest possible range – both left-hand engines and the inner wing soon began to burn. During my exit to the right, I rammed the tail assembly of another Boeing and had to bail out. From my parachute I observed the Boeing I had attacked going down steeply, and at an altitude of 4000 metres its left wing came away. Seven men bailed out with parachutes.'

The first B-17 came down near the village of Hilbeck, east of Unna, while the Flying Fortress Blech collided with crashed in the same area. He landed by parachute near Altenbögge.

Meanwhile, Unteroffizer Heinz Weber of 5./JG 1 had targeted 'the fourth aircraft from the left' in the *Pulk*. The B-17 quickly started 'to trail flames from the left wingroot and the left-hand inner engine. The blaze grew big very quickly'. Weber was credited with his second victory, but as he made his exit he was attacked by Thunderbolts, which forced him to bail out of his Fw 190A-8 'Black 8'.

II./JG 1 accounted for three of the eight B-17s that were destroyed in the action by both *Gruppen*, while pilots from II. *Gruppe* also claimed four P-47s. In addition to the loss of Blech's and Weber's aircraft, Gefreiter Heinrich Born of 4. *Staffel* was shot down and killed in combat with the escorts, while his *Staffelkamerad*, *Unteroffizier* Johann Froschhauer, was also shot down and badly wounded.

The day's action was still not quite over for II./JG 1. As the unit reassembled at Störmede that evening, a lone B-24 straggler, trailing smoke, was spotted flying to the northwest of the airfield. Despite the lateness of the day, it was a tempting target. At 1953 hrs Bär and Schuhmacher took off to administer the *coup de grâce*. Bär approached from behind and opened fire at 400 metres, closing to 100. The Liberator suddenly jettisoned its bombs and four men were seen to bail out. Seconds later flames erupted along the fuselage, the aircraft veered to the left and exploded in mid-air, with the wreckage raining down in the area north of Ahlen. Heinz Bär had just scored his 200th victory.

On 24 April the Eighth Air Force launched a major strike on airfields and aircraft industry targets in southern Germany involving 716 bombers accompanied by 867 fighters. The Luftwaffe sent up 18 day fighter *Gruppen* to engage, and those of JG 1 would again operate independently of each other. Shortly after 1130 hrs, II. *Gruppe* was scrambled, led by Georg-Peter Eder, and assembled into battle formation over Paderborn before heading towards Darmstadt. At 1240 hrs a vast inward armada of 400-500 bombers was sighted with strong fighter escort at 6000 metres. Contact was made five minutes later with a *Pulk* of about 70-80 B-17s, and in one attack Oberfeldwebel Georg Hutter, who had joined the *Gruppe* in 1942 and who was leading 4. *Staffel* in the air, opened fire from head-on at 600 metres, closing to 200. He saw hits strike both left-side engines, which began to trail smoke, and the bomber fell back 500-800 metres behind the rest of the formation. Enemy fighters prevented him from observing the fate of the Boeing, however, and he claimed an HSS as his 14th victory.

Meanwhile, Eder shot down a B-17 over Hagenau for his 40th victory. He was to be successful again on 29 April when Berlin was to be the target once more. The Eighth Air Force committed 368 B-17s and 210 B-24s for its attack on the German capital, whilst 38 B-17s were to strike various targets of opportunity in the Berlin and Magdeburg areas. Escort was to be provided by 814 fighters. To meet the Americans, I. *Jagdkorps* was ready to deploy 275 single- and twin-engined fighters.

At 0940 hrs 27 Fw 190s of II./JG 1 were given the *Alarmstart* and, led by Major Bär, assembled with the other *Gruppen* of the *Geschwader* over Paderborn. The formation firstly made for Kassel, but was then directed towards Braunschweig to intercept an incoming force of 200 *Viermots* heading east past Hannover with escorts. At 1055 hrs JG 1 intercepted the enemy at an altitude of 7500 metres in the Braunchsweig area. Because of the strength of the escort, the *Geschwader* was forced to break up, and combat ensued in *Rotten* and *Schwärme*, although II. *Gruppe* was initially able to make a *Gruppe*-strength frontal attack on a *Pulk* of 60 Flying Fortresses and Liberators.

At 1058 hrs, Georg-Peter Eder, leading 6./JG 1, targeted a Boeing to the right of the formation and opened fire from 600 metres. He observed hits on the left wing, then the bomber entered into a spin and the left wing broke away. The B-17 crashed into Braunschweig. *Schwarmführer* Kurt Brodbeck in Fw 190A-8 'Yellow 1', also of 6. *Staffel*, fired at a bomber, striking the cabin area, the left wing and the inner port engine. The stricken engine burst into flames and began to trail thick smoke. The B-17 then rolled over to the left and fell away from the formation. It too crashed in the Braunschweig area.

Within the space of eight minutes, I. and II./JG 1 had shot down or 'cut out' eight B-17s and one B-24. II. *Gruppe* lost two pilots, including Eder's wingman, Obergefreiter Werner Triebel. Low on fuel and ammunition, the unit's aircraft landed at various airfields between Braunschweig and Berlin either singly or in *Rotten*.

Hauptmann Rüdiger Kirchmayr, the 23-year-old Austrian leader of 5./JG 1 with 13 kills to his credit, found himself at Salzwedel following the morning mission in his Fw 190A-7 'Black 1'. As he recorded;

'I took off at 1245 hrs with a *Schwarm* from Salzwedel, heading for outward-bound bomber units flying on a west-northwest course. In Grid GB I caught sight of around 200 B-17Fs and Liberators. I attacked the furthest left rearward-flying Liberator of a *Pulk* of 30-40 bombers, coming in behind it from out of the sun and opening fire from close range. The left outer engine began to burn immediately, pieces flying away from the fuselage and left wing and two crewmembers bailing out. Then the Liberator went down into a steep spiral to the right, fire spread over the whole left wing and another three crewmembers bailed out. The impact of the Liberator followed, close to a small village east of Fallersleben and north of the canal, at 1310 hrs.'

Two minutes later, Kirchmayr flew over a *Pulk* of B-17s at 5500 metres, with the sun still behind him. He opened fire on a bomber to the left of the formation;

'Following the first burst the left inner engine remained in place, a crewmember bailed out with a parachute and the Boeing veered down steeply to the left and out of formation. Shortly after, two more crewmembers jumped out with parachutes and the left wing of the Boeing began to burn fiercely. The aircraft fell steeply and disappeared into clouds.'

It is believed that the bomber crashed around Fallersleben, the kill being witnessed by Feldwebel Arnold Jansen of 5. *Staffel*. Kirchmayr was awarded his 14th and 15th victories, adding two more to II./JG 1's tally of eight *Viermots* that day.

On 11 August 1944 Kirchmayr suffered a head injury when P-51s attacked his Fw 190 in France as he was landing. On 19 September he was posted to *Stab*/JG 11 and then assumed command of I./JG 11 on 25 November, which he led until his posting to Adolf Galland's Me 262-equipped JV 44. By war's end, Kirchmayr had flown nearly 400 missions and had been accredited with 46 victories, including as many as 14 four-engined bombers (including two on one day on 6 March and 8 May 1944). He was duly awarded the Knight's Cross for this success in February 1945.

Altogether, the Berlin raid had cost the Americans 38 B-17s and 25 B-24s, with a total of 18 crewmen killed and 606 missing. The war diary of I. *Jagdkorps* recorded;

'In spite of good visibility and high numerical strength, the large-scale attack on Berlin was, for the American Air Force, no success of great importance in respect to the overall war effort. Industry in Berlin sustained only slight damage. Damage to buildings and the loss of personnel was not heavy. The strafing attacks on airfields showed no results.'

The German press was quick to exploit what had been perceived as a failure for the Eighth Air Force and a victory for the Luftwaffe. 'One of the biggest air battles ever fought!' proclaimed a Luftwaffe reporter. 'US fighters inferior to Messerschmitts and Focke-Wulfs. The fierce onslaught by German fighters only increased in violence when the enemy bombers reached the Berlin area'.

By mid-1944 Heinz Bär had been appointed to lead JG 3, flying regular missions against heavy bombers. On 1 January 1945, the day of Operation *Bodenplatte*, Bär led his *Geschwader* successfully to attack Eindhoven airfield in Holland, home to a number of Typhoon, Spitfire and Mustang squadrons of the 2nd Tactical Air Force. On 13 February, however, he was transferred away from operations to take command of the Me 262 training unit, III./EJG 2, in the relatively 'quiet' area of Lechfeld, in southern Germany, after which he assumed nominal command of JV 44.

Of Bär's final tally of around 220 aerial victories at war's end, as many as 22 are believed to have been USAAF Flying Fortresses and Liberators.

When summarising operations for April 1944, Generalleutnant Schmid, commander of I. *Jagdkorps*, noted that, 'The attention of all responsible commanders in the *Reichsverteidigung* was focused on only one danger – the Flying Fortresses and their bomb loads'.

Fw 190A 'Yellow 13' prepares to start up at Störmede in the spring of 1944. It is believed that this aircraft may have been one of those flown by Hauptmann Rüdiger Kirchmayr, *Staffelkapitän* of 5./JG 1 and victor over 14 four-engined bombers

COLOUR PLATES

1
Bf 109F-4 'Black Chevron and Bars' of Major Walter Oesau, *Geschwaderkommodore* JG 2, Beaumont le Roger, France, April 1942

2
Fw 190A-4 'Double White Chevron' of Hauptmann Egon Mayer, *Gruppenkommandeur* III./JG 2, Brittany, France, late 1942/early 1943

3
Fw 190A-6 'Brown 1' of Hauptmann Johannes Naumann, *Staffelkapitän* 6./JG 26, Lille-Vendeville, France, July 1943

4
Bf 109G-6 Wk-Nr. 18 216 'Black 10' of Feldwebel Hans-Gerd Wennekers, 5./JG 11, Mönchen-Gladbach, Germany, June 1943

5
Bf 109G-6 'White 10' of Leutnant Franz Ruhl, *Staffelkapitän* 4./JG 3, Schiphol, Holland, winter 1943/44

6
Bf 109G-6 'White 10' of Oberleutnant Alfred Grislawski, 1./JG 50, Wiesbaden-Erbenheim, Germany, late September 1943

7
Bf 109G-6 Wk-Nr. 18 105 'Black 12' of Unteroffiziere Karl-Heinz Böttner and Helmut Schwarzenhölzer, 8./JG 77, Chilivani, Sicily, July 1943

8
Bf 109G-6 'Double Black Chevron' of Hauptmann Karl Rammelt, *Gruppenkommandeur* II./JG 51, Udine, Italy, December 1943

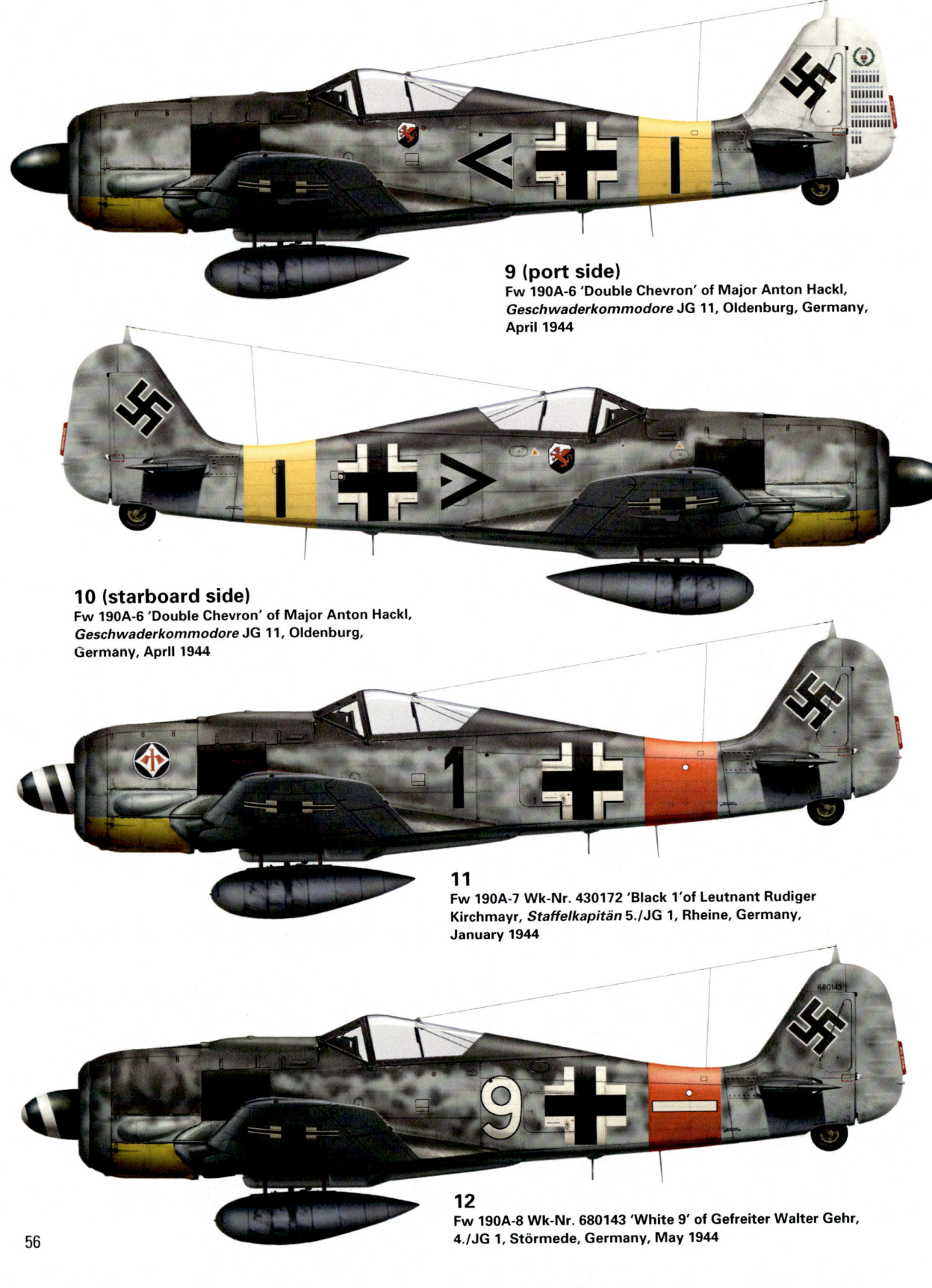

9 (port side)
Fw 190A-6 'Double Chevron' of Major Anton Hackl, *Geschwaderkommodore* JG 11, Oldenburg, Germany, April 1944

10 (starboard side)
Fw 190A-6 'Double Chevron' of Major Anton Hackl, *Geschwaderkommodore* JG 11, Oldenburg, Germany, April 1944

11
Fw 190A-7 Wk-Nr. 430172 'Black 1' of Leutnant Rudiger Kirchmayr, *Staffelkapitän* 5./JG 1, Rheine, Germany, January 1944

12
Fw 190A-8 Wk-Nr. 680143 'White 9' of Gefreiter Walter Gehr, 4./JG 1, Störmede, Germany, May 1944

13
Fw 190A-7 'Yellow 5' of 6./JG 1, Störmede, Germany, May 1944

14
Fw 190A-7 'Red 22' of Oberfeldwebel Leo Schuhmacher, *Gruppenstab* II./JG 1, Störmede, Germany, April 1944

15
Bf 110G-2 3U+KR of 7./ZG 26, Königsberg-Neumark, Germany, late 1943/early 1944

16
Bf 110G-2/R3 2N+EM of 4./ZG 76, Königsberg-Neumark, Germany, early 1944

17
Me 210A-0(1) Wk-Nr. 2100110049 2N+FR of
7./ZG 1, Wels, Austria, early 1944

18
Me 410A-1/U4 Wk-Nr. 420481 3U+LP of 6./ZG 26,
Königsberg-Neumark, Germany, April 1944

19
Me 410A-1/U4 WNr. 420292 3U+CC of Stab II./ZG 26,
Königsberg-Neumark, Germany, May 1944

20
Bf 109G-2 'Yellow 6' of Feldwebel Albert Palm, 3./JG 4, Mizil, Rumania, August 1943

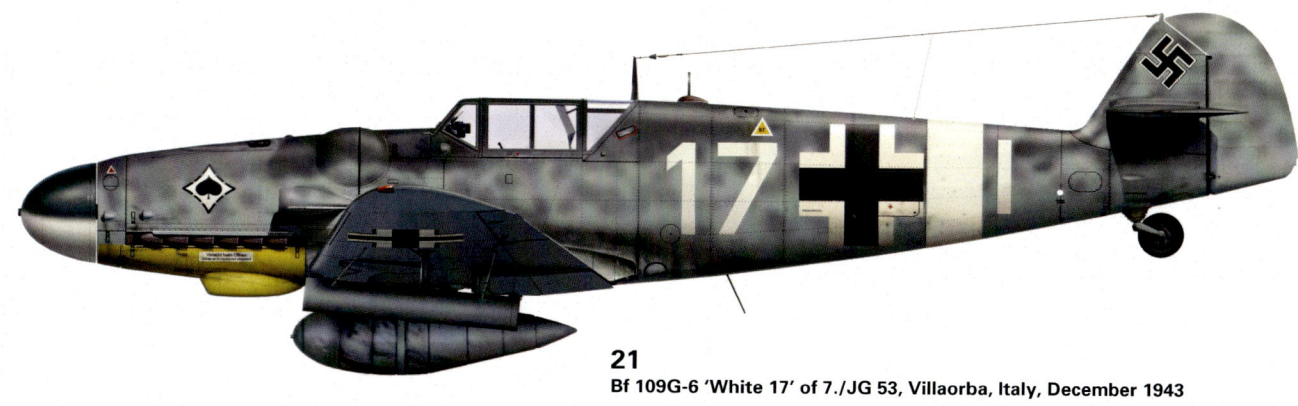

21
Bf 109G-6 'White 17' of 7./JG 53, Villaorba, Italy, December 1943

22
Bf 109G-6 'White 8' of I./JG 27, Fels am Wagram, Austria, early 1944

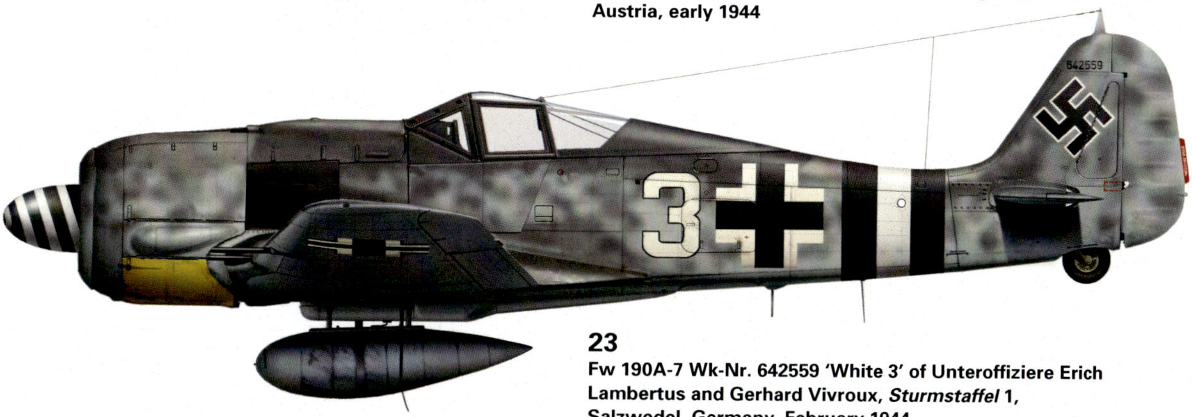

23
Fw 190A-7 Wk-Nr. 642559 'White 3' of Unteroffiziere Erich Lambertus and Gerhard Vivroux, *Sturmstaffel* 1, Salzwedel, Germany, February 1944

24
Fw 190A-8/R2 'Yellow 17' of Unteroffizier Willi Unger, 12./JG 3, Barth, Germany, May 1944

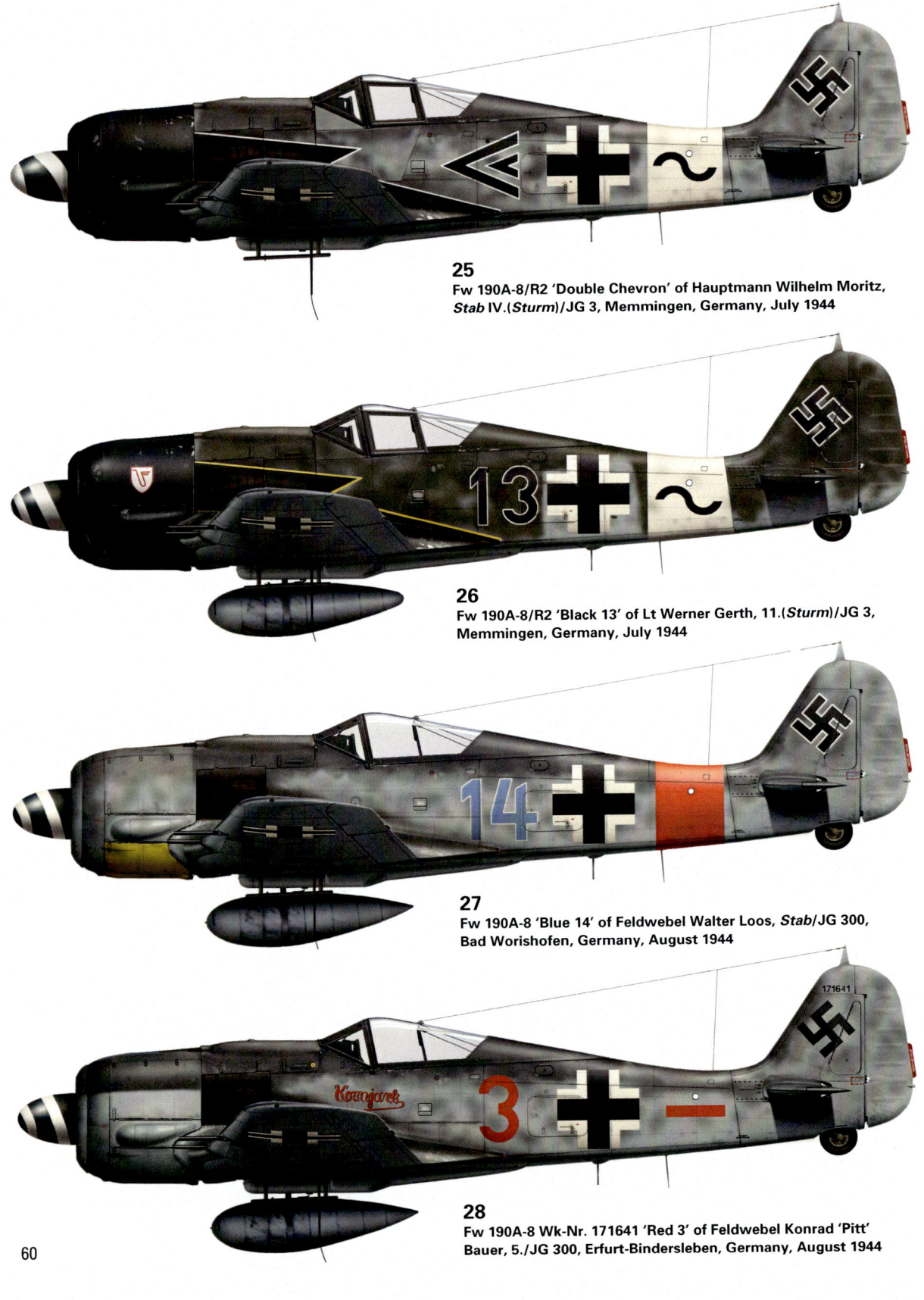

25
Fw 190A-8/R2 'Double Chevron' of Hauptmann Wilhelm Moritz, *Stab* IV.(*Sturm*)/JG 3, Memmingen, Germany, July 1944

26
Fw 190A-8/R2 'Black 13' of Lt Werner Gerth, 11.(*Sturm*)/JG 3, Memmingen, Germany, July 1944

27
Fw 190A-8 'Blue 14' of Feldwebel Walter Loos, *Stab*/JG 300, Bad Worishofen, Germany, August 1944

28
Fw 190A-8 Wk-Nr. 171641 'Red 3' of Feldwebel Konrad 'Pitt' Bauer, 5./JG 300, Erfurt-Bindersleben, Germany, August 1944

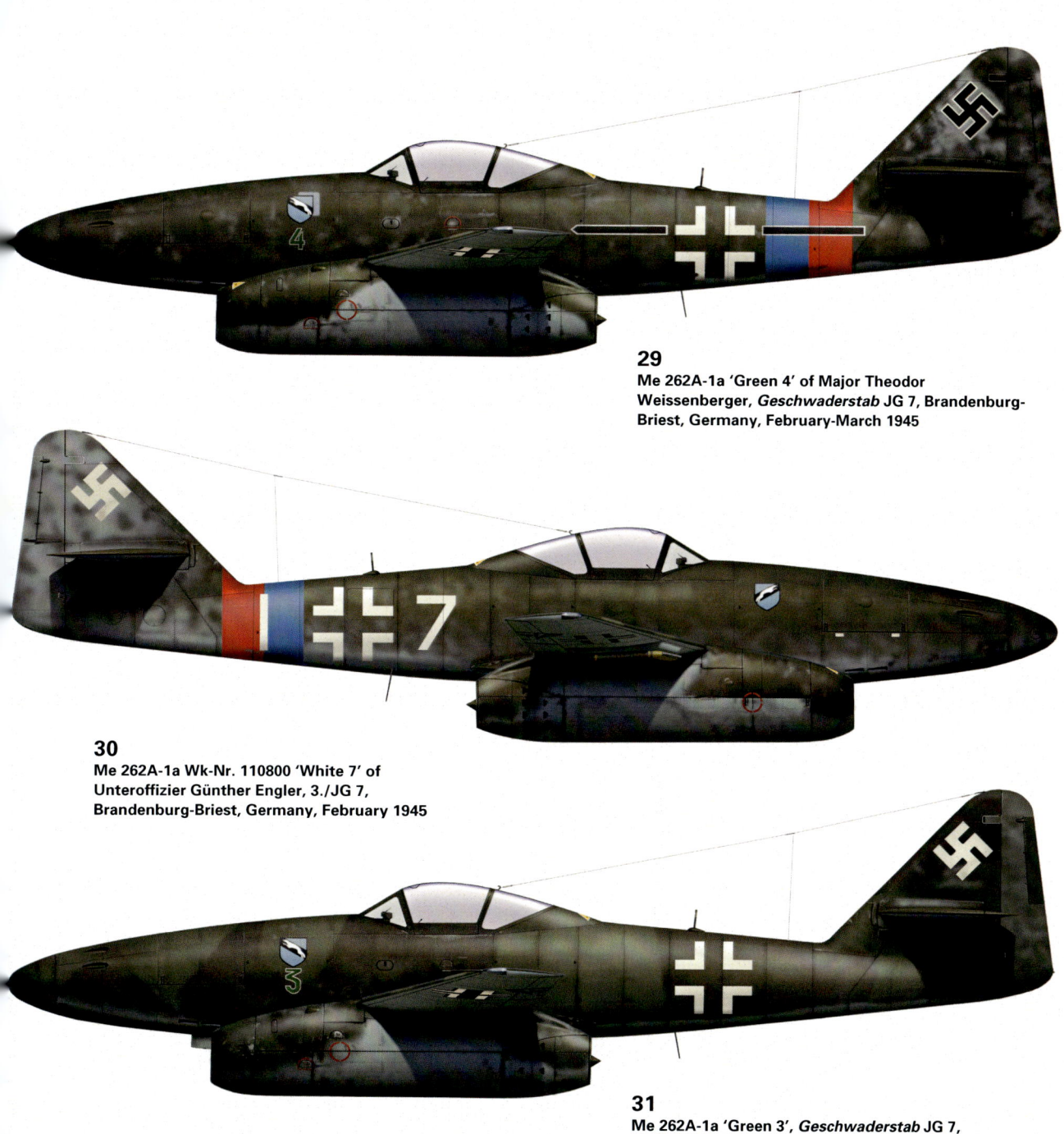

29
Me 262A-1a 'Green 4' of Major Theodor Weissenberger, *Geschwaderstab* JG 7, Brandenburg-Briest, Germany, February-March 1945

30
Me 262A-1a Wk-Nr. 110800 'White 7' of Unteroffizier Günther Engler, 3./JG 7, Brandenburg-Briest, Germany, February 1945

31
Me 262A-1a 'Green 3', *Geschwaderstab* JG 7, Brandenburg-Briest, Germany, February-March 1945

CHAPTER FIVE

'STOVEPIPES' AND DESTROYERS

The deployment of Messerschmitt Bf 110, Me 210 and Me 410 twin-engined heavy fighters – or *Zerstörer* (destroyers) – in the *Reichsverteidigung* was founded, essentially, on expediency. At the end of July 1943, having been engaged in bombing and ground-attack operations over Sicily since being pulled out of Tunisia in May, the Bf 110s of III./ZG 26 were moved from Ciampino, near Rome, back to Quakenbrück, in northern Germany. While in Africa, the *Gruppe* had sparred with B-24s in some of the first contacts with American *Viermots*, and had achieved sporadic successes. In October 1943, III./ZG 26 was joined by II./ZG 1, which had been transferred to Wels, in Austria, from the Bay of Biscay, where the unit's Bf 110s had made little impact in the anti-shipping war. From the Eastern Front, where it had been deployed on ground-attack and tank-busting operations at Kursk, I./ZG 1 arrived at Wünstorf in July.

The plan was to urgently 'refresh' these units and implement a process of transition from ground-attack and bomber escort to operations against the rapidly increasing threat of USAAF four-engined bombers. Senior figures, including Reichsmarschall Göring, believed that the Bf 110 and the new Me 410 would have the extended range needed to fight long air battles against the *Viermots*, as well as being able to serve as a capable platform to carry the heavier armament required to 'destroy' bombers when enemy escort fighters were not present.

To do this, two *Zerstörer* schools provided newly-trained crews, and an entirely new *Geschwader* was formed at the end of August 1943 with three *Gruppen* in the shape of ZG 76, its ranks drawn from various reconnaissance, nightfighter and school units. By mid-November, the *Zerstörer* units could field 340 Bf 110s, but achieving adequate training was still a challenge.

In terms of armament, the Bf 110G-2, which had entered frontline service in May 1942, carried a standard fitting of four forward-firing 7.9 mm MG 17s and a pair of 20 mm MG 151 cannon, but the two underwing bomb racks could each be replaced with a weapons tray containing a pair of MG 151s. This was supplemented by a twin 7.92 mm MG 81Z installation in the rear cockpit.

The Me 410, which superseded the problematic Me 210, reached the Luftwaffe in January 1943, and by year-end some 460 machines had been delivered, with II./ZG 26 re-equipping from the Me 210 in September. The Me 410 could be adapted to accept a wide range of armament options for anti-bomber work, but in its basic form the aircraft was fitted with two forward-firing MG 17s and two MG 151s, with single 13 mm MG 131 machine guns in rearward-firing remotely-controlled barbettes on either side of the fuselage.

An Me 210A-1 of ZG 26 seen at Diepholz, in Germany, in August 1943 following its return to the Reich from North Africa. The aircraft has been adapted for its new home defence role by the fitting of underwing twin 21 cm WGr mortar tubes intended for breaking up enemy bomber *Pulks*

From a tactical perspective, the real value in the *Zestörer* came in their ability to fire heavier weapons, such as large calibre cannon and air-to-air mortars. In the case of the latter, admittedly, these had not been restricted to use on twin-engined fighters, but the *Zerstörer* were able to carry heavier weapons loads than the single-engined machines. In early June 1943, upon orders from the *General der Jagdflieger*, 30 21 cm *Nebelwerfer* 42 mortar tubes, together with 200 mortar shells, were issued to I./JG 1 in Holland, with a further 34 tubes and 200 shells going to II./JG 26 in France.

Designed as an infantry weapon for use in ground warfare, the intention was to suspend the 1.3-metre-long rifled mortars from lugs under the wings of Fw 190s for use as an air-to-air weapon against formations of four-engined bombers. The theory was that the blast effect from a 112-kg shell with its 40-kg warhead exploding within the confines of a formation would scatter the *Viermots*, thus weakening their defensive firepower and rendering individual bombers more vulnerable to attack. The mortars were controlled from a cockpit armament panel and a Revi 16B reflector sight. Spin-stabilised shells were fired simultaneously when the pilot depressed a button on his control column, and in an emergency, the launching tube could be jettisoned by activating an electrically-primed explosive charge, which severed the central hook.

The mortar shells were fitted with a time fuse, pre-set at 800 metres prior to delivery to an operational unit and not subsequently adjusted. The firing range was therefore invariable, and the weapon's low velocity meant that to be effective it had to be aimed 60 metres above its target, and a shell had to detonate within 28 metres of a bomber.

Redesignated the *Werfergranate* (WGr) 21, but less formally known as 'stovepipes' because of the shape of the tubes, initial experiments with the weapon were conducted by *Zerstörer* ace Hauptmann Eduard Tratt, the *Kommandeur* of *Erprobungskommando* 25. Seconded to I./JG 1, he was assigned four Fw 190A-4s specifically to carry out the task.

At JG 26, 5.*Staffel* was assigned to conduct similar experiments. Firing practice took place over the North Sea, and on 13 June three B-17s were claimed by mortars over the German Bight, while on the 22nd, two pilots from I./JG 1 claimed a further two *Viermots* shot down and two damaged. These initial results proved sufficiently satisfactory for trials to continue using Fw 190s of both JG 1 and JG 26, as well as Ekdo 25 at Achmer and the *Erprobungsstelle* at Tarnewitz.

The weapon was used in numbers for the first time operationally on 28 July 1943 during a raid to Kassel and Oschersleben, and results were acceptable in as much as blast fragmentation did break up the bombers and a number were claimed destroyed as an indirect result. In a report prepared in late August 1943, the Headquarters of the Eighth Air Force warned, 'It would appear to be the most dangerous single obstacle in the path of our bomber offensive'.

The WGr 21 was perhaps used to its greatest effect against the Schweinfurt raid on 14 October 1943, when 62 bombers were shot down, many as a result of being dispersed from their formations by mortar shells. Mortars were also fitted to Bf 109G-6s of IV./JG 3, I., II. and III./JG 53, I. and III./JG 77 and I./JG 5 and used to varying effect in the Mediterranean and over Rumania from August 1943 until early 1944. Other Bf 109s of 7./JG 3, 5./JG 11, 2./JG 27 and 6./JG 51 so-equipped operated in the defence of the Reich, while a small number of Bf 110G-2/R-3 *Zerstörer* of ZG 76 and Me 410A/Bs of ZG 26 carried pairs of twin mortar sets in addition to an array of cannon and machine guns, operating as heavily-armed bomber-destroyers.

Although further trials continued until mid-1944, with the aim of improving the WGr 21, it was found that the launch tubes robbed German fighters – particularly the heavier *Zerstörer* – of their performance and made them vulnerable to Allied fighters. Luftwaffe commanders recognised the psychological effect of the mortars on bomber crews, but equally that when fitted to a single-engined fighter, a loss in speed of 40-50 km/h was incurred, plus a loss of ceiling and manoeuvrability. There was also a lack of a range-measuring device, and therefore an inability to control the point of detonation. Over the Italian front on 30 January 1944, the *Staffelkapitän* of 2./JG 77, Hauptmann Armin Köhler, flying a Bf 109, recorded how on one mission against US bombers over Udine, 'I took hits in the starboard wing and the (WGr 21) tube was shot away'. The next day, when the Allied bombers returned, Köhler complained that 'The mortars overshot'.

In the early stages of their deployment as bomber-destroyers in the second half of 1943, the Bf 110s of ZG 1, ZG 26 and ZG 76 enjoyed a comparatively 'safe' operational environment, free from fighter escort, during the USAAF deep penetration raids. Where possible, individual *Gruppen* would be based on airfields close to each other, and upon receiving an *Alarmstart*, each *Gruppe* of about 20-30 aircraft would take off in *Schwärme*. The *Gruppe* would then assemble in a column of *Staffeln* during a wide left-hand curve over the airfield,

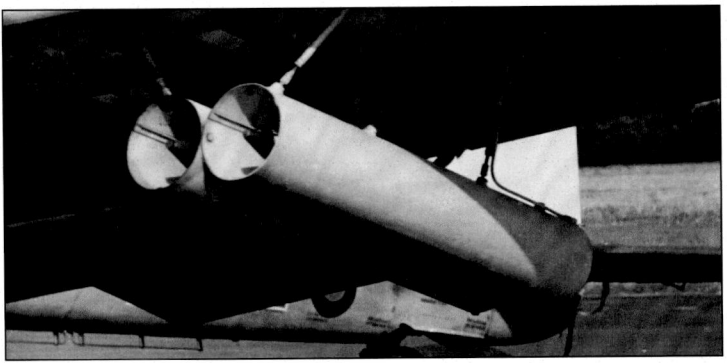

Two 21 cm WGr air-to-air mortar tubes suspended beneath the wing of an Me 410. The fuse tips of the loaded shells are visible. The mortar was adapted from an infantry weapon, and was designed to blow up individual bombers through blast or scatter their formations to break down cohesion and defensive firepower

A pair of Bf 110G-2 *Pulkzerstörer* of 3./ZG 76, fitted with underwing twin 21 cm WGr mortar tubes for breaking up enemy bomber formations. Although enjoying the relative comfort of being able to fire such weapons from a distance, in reality, the slow Bf 110s were relatively easy prey for Allied fighter escorts

and then climb to the *Geschwader* assembly point, located either over a prominent geographical point or, in bad weather, over a radio beacon. At the assembly point the aircraft formed into a column of *Gruppen*.

Upon sighting enemy bombers, the Bf 110s would deploy into a line in which the stepping up of the *Gruppen* was crucial if WGr 21 mortars were to be fired. Upon orders from the formation leader over the R/T, the *Zerstörer* crews discharged their mortars, which took place at a range of 730-900 metres, before closing up again and mounting a close-range attack using cannon and machine guns. The column formation was then resumed and the *Geschwader* made for home. In frontal or side attacks, overshooting was the common tendency, while in the case of rearward-mounted attacks, undershooting was frequent. The most practical and ballistically perfect method of attack was from dead astern.

Such was indeed the case on 10 October 1943, when the *Kommodore* of ZG 26, Major Karl Boehm-Tettelbach, led his Bf 110s, together with Me 410s of III./ZG 1, against B-17s of the 3rd BD during the attack on the marshalling yards at Münster (see Chapter Two). The division, left without any escort due to bad weather over England, had already been mauled by single-engined fighters, but the 14th BW had been particularly badly hit near Münster when the *Zerstörer* made a mass attack from the rear, inflicting considerable damage. As the American post-mission synopsis recorded;

'The fighters appeared to stay out of range, Me 110s firing at the formation with long-range weapons slung under each wing and lobbing explosive. Ju-88s [sic] attacked from 800-1000 yards, firing rockets from under each wing (two distinct puffs were seen from each ship). Their formation resembled our defensive formation.'

Blast and fragmentation from a 21 cm WGr mortar shell has damaged a B-17 during a frontal attack by Bf 110s of I./ZG 26 in the summer of 1944

Hauptmann Peter Jenne of 1./ZG 26 ranks alongside Leutnant Rudolf Dassow, also of ZG 26, as one the two highest-scoring *Zerstörer* pilots against four-engined day bombers with 12 such victories out of a total of at least 17. Jenne claimed two B-24s shot down on 22 December 1943 – a feat he repeated on 17 December the following year

Furthermore, Bf 110s were seen to '… hit a B-17 by rocket, tail came off, plane broke in two. It then collided with another B-17 near Saerbeck. Both went down. No chutes'.

Nine *Zerstörer* were lost during the Münster raid, and this was exceptional – losses usually ran at 5-10 per cent per mission. Success levels were considered good not just if bombers were shot down, but also where formations were scattered and disorganised, leaving them prey to the single-engined *Jagdgruppen*.

In the early afternoon of 22 December 1943, Oberleutnant Peter Jenne of 1./ZG 26 shot down a B-24 of the 2nd BD over the island of Texel, in Holland, following an Eighth Air Force raid on Bremen. A second Liberator followed 30 minutes later over Bolsward. Jenne had destroyed a B-17 two days earlier for his first *Viermot* kill. Commencing his flying career with 1./ZG 1 in Russia in the summer of 1942, he had flown ground-attack operations in which he destroyed 12 tanks, ten artillery pieces and eight rocket launchers. On 9 October 1943, by which time his *Staffel* had been redesignated 1./ZG 26 and was flying defensive missions over the Reich, Jenne was appointed *Staffelkapitän*. On 10 February 1944 he is known to have claimed at least one more B-17, and he may well have scored additional victories while flying the Bf 110.

In July 1944 1./ZG 26 was redesignated 1./JG 6, and Jenne converted to the Fw 190. He was appointed *Staffelkapitän* of 12./JG 300 in September and *Gruppenkommandeur* of III./JG 300 on 1 January 1945. Jenne received the Knight's Cross on 2 February in recognition of his 17th victory, but he was killed in action flying a Bf 109G-10 during an engagement with enemy fighters over Schmerwitz on 2 March. He is known to have accounted for at least 12 *Viermots*.

Towards the end of 1943 the presence of American escort fighters became a problem, and tactics were adapted accordingly. There was an attempt to loosely assign one fighter *Gruppe* to each *Zerstörergruppe*. For operations where escort was anticipated, the *Zerstörer* units often removed their underwing mortar tubes in order to increase manouevrability. Where coordination worked, the assigned *Jagdgruppe*, whose leader would be in contact with the *Zerstörer* leader, would fly close escort to the *Zerstörer*, with two *Staffeln* flying in *Schwärme* to each side and behind, while the third *Staffel* flew as top cover, 1800 metres higher. During early operations, the fighters were ordered not to attack the bombers until the *Zerstörer* had undertaken their attack.

The *Zerstörer* would then attack head-on in a column of *Schwärme*. After passing through the enemy formation once from the front, the next *Pulk* back would be attacked in a similar way, or the *Zerstörer* would curve back in and attack it from the rear, continuously in *Schwärme*.

Such partnerships was especially successful between I./ZG 26 and the Bf 109s of Günther Specht's II./JG 11, as well as between II./ZG 26 and Walther Dahl's III./JG 3.

Eduard Tratt was probably the most successful *Zerstörer* pilot of the war. He joined the Luftwaffe as a *Fahnenjunker* (officer cadet) in 1937 and went on to serve with 1./ZG 1 during the Polish campaign, in which he was promoted to leutnant. Over Dunkirk on 1 June 1940 he was able to shoot down three Hurricanes. In July 1940 Tratt was assigned to 1./*Erprobungsgruppe* 210, and flew many missions over England. The unit was subsequently renamed 1./SKG 210 and moved to the Eastern Front. There, Tratt was not only successful in ground-attack operations, destroying 24 tanks, he also shot down 20 aircraft. In January 1942 he joined 4./ZG 26 and in March was made *Staffelkapitän* of 6./ZG 26. Tratt led 2./ZG 2 from 1 May 1942, and then held the same position with 1./ZG 1 as of 27 July 1942. He received the Knight's Cross on 12 April 1942 after 20 aerial victories. On 30 January 1943 Tratt was badly wounded in a crash caused by engine failure, his radio operator being killed and his Bf 110G-2 written off.

After his recovery he was appointed *Kommandeur* of *Erprobungskommando* 25, the weapons-testing and evaluation unit that played a key role in the development of the *Reichsverteidigung*, especially in the battle against the *Viermots*. On 11 October 1943 Tratt was named *Kommandeur* of the Me 410-equipped II./ZG 26. His 30th (29 November 1943) and 38th (20 February 1944) victories were B-17s. This total made Tratt the highest scoring *Zerstörer* pilot. On 22 February his Me 410A-1 was shot down over Nordhausen and he and his gunner, Oberfeldwebel Gillert, were killed. Tratt was promoted to major posthumously.

Another notable heavy weapon that appeared in the armoury of the Me 410 was the 5 cm BK 5 cannon, adapted from a tank cannon.

Hauptmann Eduard Tratt (left), the *Gruppenkommandeur* of II./ZG 26, clad in a captured British leather flying jacket, talks with one of his pilots on 22 February 1944. Tratt ranks as the most successful *Zerstörer* pilot of the war with 38 victories, which include four four-engined aircraft. The day this photograph was taken, however, Tratt was shot down and killed while in combat with B-17s

Me 410B-1/U4s of 5./ZG 26 gathered at Königsberg-Neumark in the spring of 1944. The aircraft are fitted with the long-barrelled 5 cm BK 5 cannon, a weapon adapted from a tank gun. It was known that when used effectively, a hit with one 5 cm round was enough to bring down a heavy bomber

The Luftwaffe Technical Office had issued a requirement for a gun with a muzzle velocity of at least 600 m/sec, with a rate of of fire of 300 rounds/min. A hit with one 5 cm round was thought to be enough to bring down a bomber. Following three months of testing, during which various belt-feed and jamming malfunctions had been ironed out, the resulting weapon was fitted to aircraft of II./ZG 26 from early February 1944. By the 8th, 5. *Staffel* had 12 aircraft equipped with the cannon, and trial operations duly commenced over southern Germany and Austria.

On 22 February, during a major raid involving nearly 1400 bombers from the Eighth and Fifteenth Air Forces against targets across Germany (see Chapter Three), the *Staffelkapitän*, Oberleutnant Fritz Stehle, led ten Me 410A-1/U4s from Oberpfaffenhofen against 183 Flying Fortresses and Liberators of the Fifteenth Air Force that were heading for Regensburg. Shortly before 1300 hrs, Feldwebel Baunicke opened fire with his cannon and shot down the BK 5's first bomber. Around ten minutes later, Stehle claimed another south of Dachau.

On 24 February, the crew of Oberfeldwebel Willi Frös and Unteroffizier Gerhard Brandl of 5./ZG 26 shot down a B-17 of the Fifteenth Air Force at 6000 metres over Steyr during an attack on the aircraft plant there. Frös would be accredited with three *Viermots* shot down. More missions with the BK 5 would be flown throughout the spring and summer of 1944, but they brought virtually no success.

Also on 22 February 1944, Hauptmann Egon Albrecht, *Kommandeur* of II./ZG 1, managed to shoot down a Liberator south of Pilsen for his first four-engined victory. The next day, he claimed a second B-24 of the Fifteenth Air Force downed south of Wels, in Austria, during an attack on Steyr.

Albrecht, who had been born in Brazil, flew missions in Russia with 6./ZG 1, which subsequently became 9./ZG 76, then 6./SKG 210 and, finally, 6./ZG 1. He was appointed *Staffelkapitän* of 1./ZG 1 on 12 June 1942. By 25 May 1943 he had achieved 15 victories, and was responsible for the destruction of hundreds of enemy vehicles as well as troop and gun positions and locomotives in the East, for which he was awarded the Knight's Cross.

Leading II./ZG 1, Albrecht flew operations over the Bay of Biscay, and after defensive operations over Austria from late 1943 to mid-1944, he returned to Germany in July 1944, where his *Gruppe* converted to the Bf 109 and was redesignated as JG 76.

On 25 August, Albrecht became yet another victim of Allied air superiority when his Bf 109G-14 was shot down over Normandy by enemy fighters. He bailed out but was found dead on the ground. Albrecht was credited with 25 victories, of which

Having just returned from an operational flight, Oberfeldwebel Willi Frös of 5./ZG 26 stands on the wing root of his Me 410B-1 at Königsberg-Neumark in May 1944 to be greeted by his groundcrew. Visible is the *Zielfernrohr* 4A telescopic sight in the armoured windscreen. Frös is holding a bandolier of flare cartridges in his hand. It is believed he accounted for five *Viermots* shot down

at least six are believed to have been *Viermots*, including two B-24s in one day on 26 June 1944.

From March 1944, the sheer numbers of American escort fighters outnumbered, outgunned and outperformed the *Zerstörer*. The first major setback came on 16 March 1944 when ZG 76 lost a devastating 26 aircraft shot down by P-51s out of 43 in the air. The Mustangs had struck just as the Bf 110s were about to attack bombers in the Augsburg area, and there was no time to form a defensive circle. III./ZG 76 never flew a mission again and was disbanded. It was the beginning of the end for the *Zerstörer*.

Ten days earlier, against the Eighth Air Force attack on Berlin, the Luftwaffe had fielded a large *Gefechtsverband* comprising a lead element of 41 Bf 110s and Me 410s from II. and III./ZG 26 and I. and II./ZG 76. Many of these aircraft were equipped with underwing batteries of four 21 cm mortars that were to be used to break up the approaching enemy formation, followed by 72 Bf 109s and Fw 190s. However, Mustangs dived out of the sun to intercept the German fighters, and in doing so forced the *Zerstörer* to break off their attacks early. This caused many of the mortar shells to explode way off target. By the end of the mission, of the seven Bf 110s of III./ZG 26 that had gone into action, five had been destroyed and the remaining two damaged. Eleven further *Zerstörer* were destroyed and at least two more damaged.

But even at the eleventh hour there were isolated successes brought about by the determination of the crews. During a major attack on Budapest by the Fifteenth Air Force on 2 July 1944, having failed to form up into a *Gefechtsverband*, 20 Me 410s of I./ZG 76 nevertheless attacked a lone combat wing of B-17s and claimed 13 shot down for the loss of just one Me 410. In fact, the Fifteenth Air Force reported the loss of only four B-17s, but others were badly damaged.

This was not enough, however, and as losses began to exceed successes, from July 1944 the *Gruppen* of ZG 26 and ZG 76, as well as II./ZG 1, were converted to new single-engined fighter *Gruppen*, thus fulfilling a long-felt wish of the *Zerstörer* crews themselves.

A Bf 110G of III./ZG 26 stands ready for its 21 cm WGr mortar tubes to be rearmed

ALL-OUT DEFENCE

CHAPTER SIX

As we have already seen, the pilots of II./JG 1 fought a determined and often successful battle against the *Viermots* during April 1944. But their comrades in JG 1's other *Gruppen* were also active. Best illustrating this is Hauptmann Alfred Grislawski, who was *Staffelkapitän* of 8./JG 1. On 9 April, this illustrious fighter pilot, who had 121 victories to his name (most of them scored over the USSR while with JG 52) as well as the Knight's Cross, shot down two B-17s over Schleswig during the large attack on northeast Germany. Grislawski knew what was entailed in fighting bombers – on three previous occasions he had brought down two Boeings in one day, but had been shot down himself and forced to bail out with wounds as recently as 24 January 1944 when hit by defensive fire. But two days after his double in April, he was awarded the Oak Leaves and would go on to shoot down another three *Viermots*, taking his final total to 18.

Hauptmann Alfred Grislawski, *Staffelkapitän* of 1./JG 1, watches a mechanic work on the wing of his Fw 190A-7 'White 9' at Dortmund in January 1944. The aircraft is fitted with flame suppressors over the engine-mounted 13 mm machine guns so that it could be flown on night operations. The fighter also boasts an armoured windscreen. This Focke-Wulf would be lost on 22 February 1944 in combat with USAAF heavy bombers while being piloted by Gefreiter Alfred Martini of 2./JG 1

Also accounting for two Liberators and two Flying Fortresses in April was Leutnant Walter Köhne of 3./JG 1. Of his 30 victories, half were four-engined bombers scored between June 1943 and May 1944.

On 12 April, to the west, Feldwebel Gerhard Vogt of 7./JG 26 led the scoring when he claimed two B-24s from the 445th BG over Belgium. Awarded the Knight's Cross in November 1944, he was killed exactly a fortnight after the *Bodenplatte* New Year's Day mass fighter operation when his Fw 190D-9 was shot down by Allied fighters near Köln. Of Vogt's 48 victories, eight would be *Viermots*.

The Eighth Air Force lost 398 bombers to Luftwaffe fighters in March and April 1944, compared with 361 in the first 12 months of its operations. It seemed that the tactics adopted by the Germans were working. Indeed, the total number of combats in the first four months of 1944 was higher than any other similar period for the Eighth. One Eighth Air Force report warned, 'Even extensive escort cover cannot prevent a relatively small but determined enemy fighter force from avoiding or swamping the cover and attacking the bombers at some point on the long formation'.

The Eighth had observed that between January and May 1944 the number of tail attacks decreased, while nose attacks increased and that, 'the introduction of chin and nose turrets was not reflected by any drop in nose attacks. The trend towards nose attacks in this period may have been because these turrets had not proved as dangerous to the enemy as he had anticipated. The B-17 is apparently particularly vulnerable to nose attacks which are level or high. The B-24 shows up particularly poorly against nose attacks which are level or low – perhaps a result of fewer ball turrets being flown'.

Increasingly during the spring of 1944, the principle of the large-scale *Gefechstverband* was being adopted by the Germans as a means with which to tackle mass with mass. In this regard, the *Gruppen* of JG 3 often flew into action alongside the heavily armed and armoured Fw 190s of *Sturmstaffel* 1. On 8 April, a *Gefechtsverband* comprising *Sturmstaffel* 1 and *Stab*, I., II. and IV./JG 3 was sent up to intercept bombers northwest of Braunschweig. Launching a massed frontal attack over Fallersleben, a massive air battle commenced, the sky swirling with American fighters, Bf 109s and Fw 190s as the bombers lumbered on into their bomb run. The *Sturmstaffel* attacked a box of Liberators, and within a matter of minutes had shot down four of them, Leutnant Siegfried Müller claiming his third victory. Müller had joined the *Sturmstaffel* from II./JG 51 in Italy and went on to destroy nine four-engined bombers by the end of 1944, before joining JG 7 to fly the Me 262 in April 1945.

Meanwhile, on 15 April Galland visited the *Geschwaderstab* JG 3 and IV./JG 3 at Salzwedel, accompanied by Hauptmannn Wilhelm Moritz. Galland duly introduced him as the new *Kommandeur* of IV. *Gruppe* in place of Major Friedrich-Karl Müller, who had been promoted to *Geschwaderkommodore*. An experienced fighter pilot, Moritz had joined JG 3 from 11./JG 51 in October 1943. He assumed command of a unit that boasted many pilots with impressive victories against the *Viermots*.

One such individual was Leutnant Hans Iffland of 10./JG 3, who had shot down two Liberators on 9 April followed by a pair of Flying Fortresses on the 11th. Of Iffland's eventual 18 victories, 16 would be four-engined, before he was forced to bail out of his Fw 190 on 7 July with severe wounds that prevented his return to operations.

Leutnant Willi Unger had not long been with 11./JG 3 after completing his training when he accounted for four *Viermots* by 13 April, while his *Staffelkapitän*, Leutnant Hans Weik, had claimed no fewer than nine four-engined bombers by the end of March. In April Weik, who had previously served as an instructor, continued to demonstrate a formidable aptitude for anti-bomber operations when he shot down two B-17s on the 24th as well as claiming an HSS. Weik would end the war credited with 22 four-engined kills from a total of 36 victories.

Galland intended to convert IV./JG 3 into a fully-fledged *Sturmgruppe* that would apply the tactical doctrine of the original *Sturmstaffel* but in *Gruppe* strength. Reaction to this proposal was mixed and led to debate. Many officers felt that it was unnecessary to sign documents of obligation in the same way as the *Sturmstaffel*, let alone volunteer for tactics that would involve ramming or court-martial, when those already employed were achieving results as was demonstrated on 29 April during the USAAF attack on Berlin (see Chapter Four).

That morning, *Sturmstaffel* 1 and IV./JG 3 took off together from Salzwedel led by Weik. Once assembled with other *Gruppen* over Magdeburg, the *Gefechtsverband* headed towards Braunschweig. Shortly before 1100 hrs, the formation sighted bombers and Weik turned his aircraft to launch a frontal attack. Simultaneously, and in conformity with tactical doctrine, the *Sturmstaffel* formed up for a rearward attack on another

CHAPTER SIX

Oberfeldwebel Walter Loos in the cockpit of Fw 190A-8 'Blue 14' of *Stab*/JG 300. Loos was posted to 11./JG 3 in January 1944 and scored his first *Herausschuss* on 6 March. He would go on to account for another eight *Herausschuss* and five four-engined bombers shot down. He later moved to *Stab*/JG 300 and then *Stab*/JG 301. Loos was awarded the Knight's Cross on 20 April 1945 and of his 38 victories, 22 were *Viermots*

Eastern Front *Experte* Oberfeldwebel Helmut Rüffler of 4./JG 3 (left) commenced operations in the defence of the Reich in September 1943 and ended the war with eight confirmed four-engined kills. He is seen here posing with Gefreiter Hans Kupka and the latter's Bf 109G-6 'White 13' at Rotenburg in February 1944

part of the formation, trusting in the protection of the Fw 190's armour-plated cockpits whilst closing in to killing range.

By the time the *Gefechstverband* had finished its work, nine B-17s had gone down under the guns of IV./JG 3, including two claims from Weik and one each from Willi Unger and his comrade in 11./JG 3, Unteroffizier Walter Loos. Loos had been posted to 11./JG 3 in January 1944 and scored his first HSS on 6 March. He would go on to account for another eight HSS and five four-engined bombers shot down, including six in the month of April 1944. Loos later moved to *Stab*/JG 300, where he flew as wingman to Walter Dahl, and then *Stab*/JG 301. Of his eventual 38 victories, 22 were *Viermots*. Weik, Unger and Loos would all be awarded the Knight's Cross later in the war. For its part, the *Sturmstaffel* had accounted for a further 13 Flying Fortresses on the 29th.

The intensity of the air fighting in April 1944 saw a host of 'bomber-killers' rise to the fore. Flying alongside the aforementioned trio from IV./JG 3 on 29 April was Feldwebel Hans Schäfer of 10. *Staffel*, who 'cut out' a *Viermot* from its formation and claimed four more as either shot down or HSS during that month. Of his final score of 18 victories, 12 would be four-engined. His *Staffel*-mate, Feldwebel Walter Hagenah, downed a B-17 and claimed an HSS on the 18th over Nauen for his ninth and tenth victories. Hagenah had flown in the East with 2./JG 3 and had shot down two Il-2s within three minutes west of Stalingrad on 14 October 1942. By war's end he was flying the Me 262 with III./JG 7 and is accredited with 17 victories, including nine *Viermots*.

Others making their mark in JG 3 included Oberfeldwebel Helmut Rüffler of 4. *Staffel*, who downed a pair of Flying Fortresses on the 19th for his 57th and 58th kills. Another veteran of *Barbarossa*, Rüffler had accumulated 50 of his 88 victories in the East, including many multiple kills. His best day was 28 October 1942, when he was credited with three Il-2s and two LaGG-3s shot down that morning. Rüffler was himself shot down over Normandy following combat with P-51s on 18 July 1944 and wounded, but he returned to flying and converted onto the Me 262. The last weeks of the war found him commanding 9./JG 51, however. He is believed to have had eight four-engine victories.

Unteroffizier Oskar Bösch joined 11./JG 3 in early May when it absorbed *Sturmstaffel* 1, which he had joined just before that unit's dissolution. Bösch shot down two B-17s over Gifhorn and Helmstedt while with the *Sturmstaffel* on 29 April, the day after his (hasty) training on the Fw 190A-8! All eight of his confirmed victories in 1944 were *Viermots*, six of them B-17s and two Liberators. He recalled;

'Every day was a struggle to stay alive. We weren't after awards. The best award was to come back at the end of the day. We were outnumbered ten, sometimes twenty-to-one and we got tired, very tired, but we kept going. We had to. In the beginning, attacking bombers was almost "easy". It was exciting. Your adrenalin really pumped. Everybody had their own tactics, their own tricks, but generally we attacked from behind at about 500 metres above the formation, opening fire at 400 metres. The air was thin at 7000 metres, and often there was turbulence behind the bombers – this made our approach difficult.

Feldwebel Oskar Bösch of 14.(*Sturm*)/JG 3 stands on the wing of his Fw 190A-8/R2 'Black 14' at Schongau in August 1944. The aircraft is fitted with armoured panels on the cockpit sides and armoured glass to the canopy sides intended for defence during close-range attacks on enemy bomber formations

'We always went in line abreast. If you went in singly, all the bombers shot at you with their defensive firepower. You drew fire from the waist gunners. But as an attack *formation*, the psychological effect on the bomber gunners was much greater. First of all you tried to knock out the tail gunner. Then you went for the intersection between wing and fuselage and you just kept at it, watching your hits flare and flare again. It all happened so quickly. You gave it all you had. Sometimes, after the first attack, all your energy seemed to go. Your nerves were burnt out.'

On 29 April, IV./JG 3, under the command of Wilhelm Moritz, was officially redesignated IV.(*Sturm*)/JG 3. *Sturmstaffel* 1 was dissolved and its pilots and groundcrews formed the nucleus of 11.(*Sturm*)/JG 3, led by Leutnant Werner Gerth. The *Gruppe* replaced its Bf 109G-6s with more heavily armed and armoured Fw 190A-8s, an aircraft considered to be better suited for work as a close-range *Sturmjäger*.

The Fw 190A-8/R2 featured two MG 151 cannon installed in the wingroots and two 30 mm MK 108 cannon in the wings. The cowl-mounted MG 131 machine guns fitted to the standard A-8 were removed to reduce weight and the empty gun troughs and slots left by their removal were covered with armoured plate. Additionally, a panel of 6 mm armoured glass was mounted on each side of the cockpit canopy, and a sheet of 6 mm armour plate, extending from the lower edge of the cockpit canopy to the wing root, was mounted externally on either side of the fuselage to protect the pilot from lateral fire. Another armoured panel on the underside of the aircraft protected the pilot's seat to a point sufficiently forward to cover the feet and legs.

Another pilot to enjoy success in April 1944 was Oberfeldwebel Herbert Rollwage of 5./JG 53, who claimed six bombers. He had joined the Luftwaffe in 1936 and subsequently flown with JG 53 over the Soviet Union and the Mediterranean in 1941–42. One of his earliest encounters against B-17s over Tunisia in March 1943 saw him shot down by escorting Spitfires. From the summer of 1943, however, beginning in the air action over Sicily, Rollwage started to take his toll of heavy bombers. He was awarded the Knight's Cross in August 1944 and, promoted to leutnant, was given command of 5./JG 53. There is some debate as to Rollwage's final scores, but it is believed that he achieved between 80-100 victories of which 14 were confirmed four-engined kills.

Exceeding Rollwage's count in April was Oberleutnant Hans-Heinrich Koenig. The tenacious Koenig had lost an eye in a night engagement with an RAF bomber while flying as a nightfighter pilot with NJG 3 in June 1942. Once he had recovered, Koenig transferred to day fighters and shot down his first B-24 on 4 October of that year. Made *Staffelkapitän* of 3./JG 11, he went on to increase his score, claiming six *Viermots* in March 1944 and eight in April, including four bombers on the 29th. In May Koenig became *Kommandeur* of I./JG 11, but on the 24th, his fighter was hit by fire from a B-17 and exploded. The force of the blast ripped a wing off the bomber, and both machines crashed to the earth. Koenig was awarded the Knight's Cross posthumously with a score of 28 victories, including 20 *Viermots*.

5./JG 53's Leutnant Herbert Rollwage is adorned with a wreath as he sits in the cockpit of his Bf 109 on a Sicilian airfield following his 300th mission against the enemy on 8 August 1942, during which he shot down a Spitfire over Malta for his 29th victory. By this stage of the war Rollwage had yet to make his presence felt in the battle against the bombers, and his first such victory would not come until 9 June 1943. Rollwage survived the war, and although his confirmed kill tally is not known, he flew 664 missions in which he was credited with 71 victories. It is thought his final total may be between 80 and 85. Rollwage is believed to have accounted for at least 14 four-engined kills. He was awarded the Oak Leaves on 24 January 1945

The loss sheet for April included Hauptmann Hans Remmer, commander of 1./JG 27. He had attacked B-24s of the Fifteenth Air Force over Graz, in Austria, on the 2nd and shot one down over Jüdenburg, but his Bf 109G-6 was hit by defensive fire and upon bailing out, his parachute failed to deploy and he fell to his death. Remmer had accounted for 16 kills over North Africa, including a Brewster Buffalo, Hurricanes, Wellingtons and P-40s. In his final tally of 27 victories, nine were four-engined. He was awarded the Knight's Cross posthumously.

From JG 3, Oberleutnant Otto Wessling, *Staffelkapitän* of 11. *Staffel*, was killed on 19 April when he made an emergency landing in his burning Bf 109G-6 near Eschwege following operations against heavily escorted bombers in the Göttingen/Kassel area. He had been awarded the Knight's Cross in September 1942 and the Oak Leaves were awarded posthumously. Wessling had claimed 12 bombers in his total of 83 kills.

On 20 May 1944, Anton Hackl, *Gruppenkommandeur* of III./JG 11, informed Galland in writing of his belief that the key to tackling bombers was 'to attack as late as possible, causing bombers to jettison even though a late approach excludes the possibility of a second operation, or to attack as early as possible, thus allowing *Gruppe* after *Gruppe* to attack at minute intervals. Allied fighter relief would then be forced to deal with the main body of attacking elements, one after the other, necessitating a splitting of forces, and would not be in a position to hamper individual *Gruppen* making repeated frontal attacks'.

Since the first daylight raid on Berlin in March 1944, there had been pressure on the Jagdwaffe to improve control of its *Gruppen* based across the Reich so as to launch quick, concentrated responses to the American bombers. Galland proposed the formation of a special *Gefechtsverband* command to be known as the *Jagdgeschwader zur besonderen Verwendung* (JGzbV) that would oversee a number of *Jagdgruppen* in southern Germany, and which would operate as a cohesive force with the prime role of attacking bombers from both the Eighth and Fifteenth Air Forces.

On 23 April, Major Gerhard Michalski, the *Kommandeur* of II./JG 53 and a veteran *jagdflieger* of the Mediterranean Front who wore the Knight's

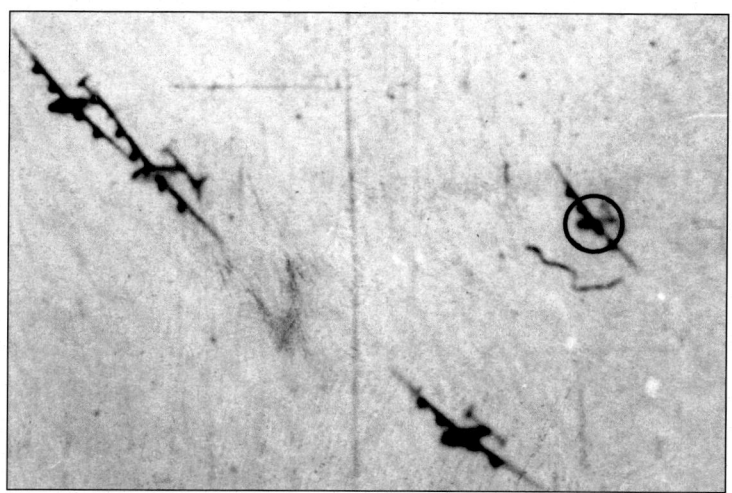

The view from the BSK 16 gun camera in the Fw 190A-8 of Oberfeldwebel Gerhard Marburg of *Sturmstaffel* 1 at the moment he made a frontal approach on a *Pulk* of B-24s at 1012 hrs on 8 May 1944 during an attack by the USAAF's 2nd BD on Braunschweig. In this still, Marburg's targeted Liberator has been ringed at a range of 200 metres. Marburg was flying at an altitude of 6500 metres at the time, closing on the B-24 before opening fire with his MG 151 20 mm cannon. He was credited with his sixth victory following this mission

Left
Hauptmann Dr Peter Werfft, *Gruppenkommandeur* of III./JG 27. He was awarded the Knight's Cross on 28 January 1945 and is credited with 24 victories, of which 14 were *Viermots*. On 19 May 1944, while *Staffelkapitän* of 9./JG 27, he shot down two B-24s east of Helmstedt for his 21st and 22nd victories, but his Bf 109G-6 was attacked by US fighters as he flew to Gardelegen to refuel and re-arm, and he was severely wounded. Werfft did not return to operational service until November, when he took over command of III. *Gruppe* from Oberleutnant Franz Stigler

Cross, was appointed to set up the *Stab* JGzbV at Kassel. Michalski had downed his first Flying Fortress over Tunisia on 2 March 1943, although it was unconfirmed. Following his return to the Reich, by the end of April 1944 he had claimed six B-17s and three B-24s destroyed. On 1 May however, just after his appointment, Michalski was wounded, and Galland asked Major Walter Dahl if he would lead the JGzbV.

Dahl, CO of Bf 109-equipped III./JG 3 (one of the most successful units in the *Reichsverteidigung*), had fought over Russia with II./JG 3 since the start of *Barbarossa*, with a brief interlude in the Mediterranean. By the spring of 1943 he had 50 victories to his credit. In the summer of 1943 Dahl took command of III./JG 3 in Russia, but in early August the *Gruppe* was posted back to Germany and engaged in Reich defence. From here on Dahl was to earn himself a formidable reputation as a tactical exponent in the war against the bombers. On 11 March he was awarded the Knight's Cross in recognition of his 64 victories, amongst which were nine B-17s.

Dahl agreed to Galland's request and put things into immediate effect. He established a headquarters for the new JGzbV at Ansbach and was assigned five *Jagdgruppen* – III./JG 3 at Ansbach, I./JG 5 (equipped with high-altitude Bf 109G-6/ASs for the escort fighter role) at Herzogenaurach, II./JG 27 at Unterschlauersbach, II./JG 53 at Frankfurt-Eschborn and III./JG 54 at Lüneburg.

Meanwhile, several senior fighter commanders were leading by example. Oberstleutnant Gustav Rödel, the *Kommodore* of JG 27 (and also a *Legion Condor* veteran and holder of the Oak Leaves to the Knight's Cross), would shoot down three bombers in May, including two B-17s on the 12th. Suriving the war with 98 victories to his name, which including 12 *Viermots*, Rödel recalled;

'I flew and survived more than 1000 missions, but attacking four-engined bombers flying in formation still remains a nightmare in my memory. Each attack had a different pattern. There were too many odds and unknown factors during an approach such as weather, the counter-action of the fighter escort and the difficulty in manoeuvring in a large formation. The sole aim of the flight leader was to get his formation into a position that allowed a virtual collision-course attack. Thereafter, it was every pilot for himself.'

On 24 May Dahl's JGzbV grouping flew its first major operation against the enemy in which a successful engagement was made against some of the 517 B-17s that set out to bomb Berlin under the cover of nearly 400 escort fighters. Bounced by P-51s over Rangsdorf, the German force, believed to have included elements of II./JG 27, II./JG 53 and III./JG 54, engaged in a vast, fighter-versus-fighter battle, although a few aircraft did manage to break through to the bombers. The Fw 190s of

A Bf 109G-6 is checked by a member of the groundcrew in its forested dispersal in the summer of 1944. The fighter is equipped with underwing 20 mm MG 151 cannon designed for use against four-engined bombers. While effective against *Viermots*, the MG 151 installation meant that the aircraft was not as adept in combat against Allied escort fighters

III./JG 54 accounted for ten B-17s (including three HSS). Thirty-three B-17s were lost and a further 256 damaged. Dahl sent an ebullient report of events to Galland.

Three days later, the 3rd BD despatched 102 B-17s to bomb aircraft industry targets and a marshalling yard at Strasbourg, in France, and a further 98 Flying Fortresses to strike a railway yard in Karlsruhe. The JGzbV ordered I./JG 5 airborne at 1100 hrs to intercept the bombers heading for Strasbourg, while at 1130 hrs III./JG 3 sent 21 Bf 109s to Karlsruhe. Oberfeldwebel Georg Ströbele claimed a B-17 destroyed and Hauptmann Karl-Heinz Langer a *Herausschuss*. Operating together, II./JG 27 and II./JG 53 engaged B-17s near Nancy. The former *Gruppe* managed to destroy two Mustangs and a B-17, while II./JG 53's Herbert Rollwage claimed one of the unit's score of three B-17s and a P-51. But II./JG 27 lost three pilots and six Bf 109s to enemy action.

Throughout May, the Luftwaffe found it increasingly difficult to concentrate its forces against large-scale American raids as its units were scattered across the Reich. This in turn meant that they had to fly great distances to reach the bombers and required long periods to assemble into *Gefechtvervbände*. Consequently, German fighters were often late in intercepting the *Viermots*, or were forced to land early as a result of fuel shortage. Willi Unger recalled;

Unteroffizier Willi Unger, an accomplished *Sturmgruppe* pilot of 12./JG 3, sits on the engine cowling of his Fw 190A-8/R2 'Yellow 17' at Barth in May 1944. The first 21 of WIII Unger's 24 confirmed victories were four-engined bombers. He was awarded the Knight's Cross on 23 October 1944

'The operational bases of our fighter units in the *Reichsverteidigung* were spread all over Germany. Attempts to maintain strength at critical times and in critical areas were made by the rapid redeployment of fighters to northern or southern Germany. Several *Gruppen* would combine together in the air from various airfields and were then led together from the ground to attack the approaching bombers. This did not always work. The bombers often "cheated", flew towards one town, then changed their course and bombed a completely different target. As the flying endurance of our fighters with an auxiliary drop tank was maximum 2.5 hours, we were often forced to break off. There is no question of German fighters having the advantage – only disadvantages, since the numbers of American escort fighters were far superior to us and they also operated at higher altitude, again to our disadvantage.'

On 29 May, in response to a raid by the Fifteenth Air Force on the Messerschmitt works at Wiener-Neustadt, a lack of radio communication within a *Gefechtsverband* comprising IV.(*Sturm*)/JG 3 and elements from JG 300, which had just started large-scale daylight operations, led to confusion and the break up of the formation. Amidst the confusion, the Bf 109G-6 flown by Major Friedrich-Karl Müller, *Kommodore* of JG 3, collided with another machine and was forced to crash-land at Salzwedel, stalling in from a height of 15 metres. 'Tutti' Müller was killed in the crash. Having flown some 600 missions, his death added to the growing list of valued formation leaders who had been killed defending the German homeland.

Müller was a veteran of the *Kanalkampf*, before being posted to Russia. In the latter theatre in mid-1942, while flying with 1./JG 53, he had enjoyed several days of multiple kills, including six Il-2s on 9 September and seven enemy aircraft in one day on the 18th. Following the award of the Oak Leaves to his Knight's Cross and a tour of duty in North Africa as *Kommandeur* of I./JG 53, the exhausted Müller was given extended leave, but on 26 February 1944 he was appointed to command JG 3 in the Reich and returned to old form. He had shot down his first B-17 over Africa on 31 January 1943, and between 6 March 1944 and 24 April 1944, all 18 of his victims were heavy bombers – eleven B-17s and seven B-24s.

Müller had been mentioned in the official *Wehrmacht* bulletin for 18 April when IV./JG 3 had claimed 19 B-17s destroyed during a raid on Berlin. In May he would shoot down another four bombers, including two on the 12th. By the time of his death Müller's tally stood at 140 victories, including 23 *Viermots*, placing him amongst the highest scorers.

Müller's successor at the head of JG 3, Wilhelm Moritz, quickly displayed a proficiency for anti-bomber work too, embarking on a run of five *Herrausschüsse* from 29 April to 13 May 1944, with two on the 8th and two on the 13th, resulting in a total of 39 victories. He was awarded the Knight's Cross on 18 July and went on to account for at least another five *Viermots* destroyed.

In the flying ranks of JG 3, Leutnant Rudolf Metz of 11. *Staffel* had excelled himself on 12 May when the USAAF bombed synthetic fuel production plants and he accounted for three HSS in eight minutes over the Nidda/Sulzbach area. Moving to 6./JG 4 on 30 July, he shot down another five *Viermots* to achieve a final score of ten victories before he was killed in action on 11 November 1944. Posthumously awarded the *Ehrenpokal* (Honour Goblet), Metz was one of a handful of pilots who held the distinction of all of their victims being four-engined bombers.

In mid-May 1944, von Kornatzki was ordered to set up II.(*Sturm*)/JG 4 at Salzwedel and Welzow. Formed around a solid core of pilots from *Sturmstaffel* 1 who understood what was required of them, the *Gruppe* had to wait until late July to

Three leading *Sturmgruppe* officers in discussion at Memmingen following the Allied bombing attacks on the airfield on 18 and 20 July 1944. From left to right are Hauptmann Heinz Lang (Chief of the *Stabskompanie*, IV./JG 3) and Majors Walter Dahl (*Kommodore* of JG 300) and Wilhelm Moritz (*Kommandeur* of IV./JG 3). Together, Dahl and Moritz would account for more than 40 *Viermots* shot down

receive its first Fw 190A-8/R2s, and for most of the summer its personnel underwent conversion and tactical training.

A third *Sturmgruppe* had also begun forming up that month when 4. and 5. *Staffeln* of the single-seat *Wilde Sau* nightfighter *Gruppe*, II./JG 300 commenced conversion to the day fighter role, together with I. and III./JG 300. II./JG 300 took delivery of Fw 190A-8/R2s, while I. and III. *Gruppen* kept their Bf 109s for the escort role.

In late June 1944 Walther Dahl relinquished command of his *Jagdgeschwader z.b.V* and was appointed *Kommodore* of JG 300. Within II./JG 300, Dahl was able to draw on a number of battle-hardened pilots, and the new *Sturmgruppe* was designated II.(*Sturm*)/JG 300 in July 1944. By 4 August, the conversion and training of the unit as a *Sturmgruppe* was complete.

Following the Allied invasion of Normandy on 6 June, the bulk of the German daylight fighter force was sent to France, but there was still the need to provide an effective defence over the Reich. Three days after the invasion, the *Wilde Sau* unit I./JG 302 clashed over Landshut with some of the 500 B-17s and B-24s of the Fifteenth Air Force that had been sent to bomb ammunition and aircraft industry targets around Munich.

Hauptmann Heinrich Wurzer, *Staffelkapitän* of 1./JG 302, shot down two B-24s from the 49th BW in 12 minutes for his 21st and 22nd victories. Indeed, Wurzer's scoring pattern had seemed founded on 'double-scores', with two *Viermots* falling to him on 6 and 8 March, 9 April and 10 and 24 May. He would continue with this pattern on 16 June and 8 July, finally claiming 23 four-engined bombers, making him one of the Jagdwaffe's top scorers.

Oberfeldwebel Artur Groß of 2./JG 302 accounted for three of the Liberators over Landshut on 9 June. Like Rudolf Metz of JG 3, all of Groß's victims (11 in total) were four-engined bombers.

Leutnant Ernst-Erich Hirschfeld of 5./JG 300, a successful *Wilde Sau* pilot, had shot down nine *Viermots* at night between August 1943 and February 1944. In June 1944 all of his seven kills were four-engined bombers, including three Liberators in one day over Berlin on the 21st and two more on the 26th. Flying on the 21st with Hirschfeld was Feldwebel Hubert Engst also of 5. *Staffel*, who brought down a pair of B-24s in ten minutes – just two of 20 *Viermots* he accounted for. Engst survived the war, but just over a month after his June 'triple', on 28 July, Hirschfeld (by then the *Staffelkapitän* of 6./JG 300, bailed out after attacking bombers near Erfurt. His parachute failed to open and he was killed. Hirschfeld had by then claimed 24 victories.

Counteracting such successes were the losses being sustained in the fighter-versus-fighter cauldron of Normandy, which included valued formation leaders and pilots who were proficient in missions against

Leutnant Rudolf Metz (left) is seen here with a member of his groundcrew whilst serving with I./JG 5 in Norway in 1943. Following a period with *Sturmstaffel* 1 in the spring of 1944, he was assigned to 11./JG 3 in May. Metz shot down three Flying Fortresses on 12 May 1944 and two Liberators on 27 September

bombers, but who had been thrown against the invasion forces. This included Austrian Leutnant Anton-Rudolf Piffer of 1./JG 1. Of his 35 victories, no fewer than 26 were four-engined bombers claimed in the 12 months between June 1943 and June 1944 – including single B-17s downed on three consecutive days in October 1943 and two in one day on 30 January 1944. 'Toni' Piffer lost his life when attacked by US fighters over France on 17 June 1944. He was awarded the Knight's Cross posthumously on 20 October.

On 7 July the Eighth Air Force sent 939 B-17s and B-24s, escorted by more than 650 fighters, to attack a range of aircraft and synthetic oil plants in central Germany, and this time the defenders would inflict a devastating blow on the Americans. At 0935 hrs, as the Liberators of the 492nd BG approached Oschersleben from the west, a *Gefechtsverband* led by Walther Dahl, comprising 44 Fw 190A-8s of Wilhelm Moritz' IV.(*Sturm*)/JG 3 from Illesheim, escorted by Bf 109G-10s from I. and III./JG 300, evaded the fighter escort and closed in on the group's Low Squadron. Initially it had been planned to make a frontal attack against the bombers, but this was changed to a rear attack, made at 0940 hrs at an altitude of 5600 metres over Oschersleben.

Despite the massed defensive fire, the Fw 190s spread across the sky line abreast in a formidable broad front and closed to 100 metres before opening fire. It took the *Sturmböcke* about a minute to shoot down 11 Liberators – an entire squadron. When the B-24s of the 2nd AD returned home, 28 of their number had been lost, most of them to the *Sturmgruppe*, which had lost nine of its own aircraft in the attack. Altogether, the Eighth Air Force lost 37 heavy bombers, with a further 390 damaged, during the day's raid.

Prominent in the attack was Leutnant Werner Gerth, *Staffelkapitän* of 11.(*Sturm*)/JG 3 (later 14.(*Sturm*)/JG 3) who claimed his 13th and 14th victories within one minute. He would down five *Viermots* during the month. In the summer of 1943 Gerth was posted to 7./JG 53 in Italy but, having recovered from wounds sustained there, he volunteered for *Sturmstaffel* 1 in January 1944, and duly became one of the unit's most successful pilots. Of Gerth's 27 confirmed victories, 22 were four-engined bombers, several of them multiple victories claimed in one day. His Fw 190A-8/R2 was hit by defensive fire from a B-17 over Halle on 2 November 1944 and he bailed out, but his parachute failed to open and he was killed. Gerth had been shot down 12 times previously and survived. He received a posthumous German Cross in Gold on 1 January 1945 and was promoted to hauptmann.

Fw 190A-8 'White 21' of Feldwebel Fritz Buchholz of II./JG 6 sits on the apron outside a hangar at Königsberg-Neumark, on the doors of which has been painted a full-size frontal rendition of a B-17. The *Gruppe* was formed from the Me 410-equipped II./ZG 26 in the summer of 1944. Buchholz had previously flown the twin-engined Me 410 fitted with the 5 cm BK cannon

Blasting a Liberator from the sky at 0942 hrs – exactly the same moment as Gerth – was Willi Unger of 12.(*Sturm*)/JG 3, who reported;

'I opened fire from 600 metres on a Liberator in the middle of the formation, and after the first burst the right wing and both right engines began to burn. With further continuous fire up to a range of 350metres, the enemy machine veered to the right. A real fireball wrapped around the fuselage as well as the right wing, the machine tilted further to the right and immediately the enemy machine burned up. I could not see the ground impact as I went to approach a second Liberator, which I attacked and shot down.'

Indeed, as Unger recorded;

'During a *Sturm* attack on a Liberator *Pulk* of some 25 machines, I was able to fire at a second Liberator flying in the right half of the *Pulk* immediately after my first shoot-down. Because of my alignment it was possible to attack the second Liberator. From about 300 metres, I opened continuous fire up to 100 metres. The hits went into the centre fuselage and tail assembly. The rear gunner was hit and pieces flew away from the tail unit. The Liberator immediately went into a downwards spiral to the right. As I made my exit past the enemy machine, two to four parachutes opened.'

The two Liberators smashed into the ground near Oschersleben at 0942 and 0943 hrs. Like Gerth, Unger had scored his 10th and 11th victories within one minute of each other.

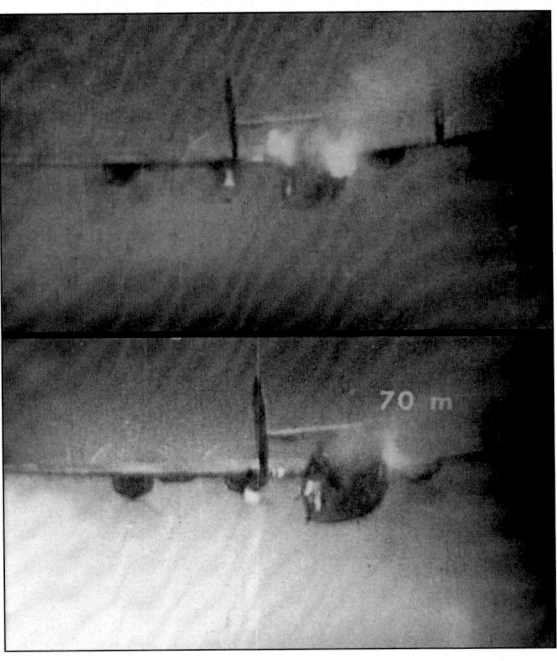

Feldwebel Otto Erhardt of 10./JG 3 brings his Fw 190A-8 in to within 70 metres of a B-24 as he presses home a rear attack during the USAAF raids on aircraft industry and synthetic oil targets on 7 July 1944. This would be Erhardt's eighth victory

On 15 August II.(*Sturm*)/JG 300 received its baptism of fire. The Eighth Air Force had used the perfect summer weather to despatch a force of nearly 900 B-17s and B-24s to bomb a range of airfield targets across Germany. At Bad Wörishofen, Walther Dahl placed his 100+ available fighters on readiness and drew up plans for a *Gefechtsverband* comprising the *Geschwaderstabsschwarm* and I./JG 300 at Bad Wörishofen (the latter unit formed of Bf 109G-10/14s in the high-altitude escort role), II.(*Sturm*)/JG 300 at Holzkirchen and IV.(*Sturm*)/JG 3 at Schongau.

Within two hours Dahl was airborne, accompanied by the 30 Bf 109s of I./JG 300 as escort. The formation headed south to Augsburg, where it made a textbook rendezvous with the 30 Fw 190s of the two *Sturmgruppen* just after 1000 hrs. Under radio silence at 7000 metres, and with Dahl at the head of a great wedge-shaped battle formation, the German fighters turned towards Frankfurt, some 260 km away. IV.(*Sturm*)/JG 3's Fw 190s were flying in two stacked down 'Vees' or '*Sturmkeil*', each – theoretically – comprised of eight to ten aircraft (depending on serviceability), the second formation flying 140-180 metres behind and about 45 metres below the lead formation.

Meanwhile, the Bf 109 escorts were split on either side of the *Sturmgruppe*, stacked up from front to rear. Another, smaller escort flew high cover some 900 metres above the rearmost aircraft of the second Vee. The Bf 109s flew in a sufficiently loose formation to avoid slipstream and allow aircraft to weave without the risk of collision.

Thirty minutes later, the fighter controllers ordered a change in course to Trier, 150 km further west. After one hour of flying in slowly deteriorating weather, the *Gefechtsverband* finally sighted three *Pulks* of 60-80 B-17s west of the Mosel River. Just before 1145 hrs, Dahl manoeuvred his *Angriffskeil* for a classic attack from the rear, with Moritz' IV.(*Sturm*)/JG 3 heading for the *Pulk* that was flying to his left and II.(*Sturm*)/JG 300, led by 5. *Staffel* commander Leutnant Klaus

Bretschneider, going for the bombers to the right. Dahl and the *Stabsschwarm* would tackle the centre *Pulk*.

Within sight of the enemy bomber formation, and some 90-150 metres above and 900-1520 metres behind it, the *Sturmgruppe* dropped its external tanks, then reformated from its Vee formation into its line abreast *Angriffsformation* (attack formation) or *Breitkeil*. This was carried out by climbing where necessary and fanning out into a slightly swept-back line abreast formation of usually more than 20 fighters, either level with or slightly above the enemy, with the commander of the *Gruppe* and his deputy flying at its apex.

In a dramatic, though somewhat embellished, account to Allied interrogators in September 1945, Dahl described a *Sturm* attack;

'Upon sighting the enemy bomber formation, the formation leader gives the signal to attack by rocking his wings or by radio. The wings of the Vics (*Keil*) now pull up until the aircraft are in line abreast, with the formation leader throttling back slightly so the others can catch up. The approach is made from behind and the fighters attack in a line, the formation leader dividing up the target according to the formation of the bombers. Open fire from the shortest possible range, about 370 metres, during the approach with all weapons simultaneously, firing bursts until close enough to ram. If no victory is yet scored, ramming should result by crashing against the bomber's tail with prop or wings.

'Exit should be made from the formation to the side and down and reassemble at the same altitude, with the bombers about 2750 metres to the side and 1000 metres below. The basic principle to be observed in reassembling is that the assembly is to be made on the same side from which the entry into the bomber stream was made. The advantage thus gained is that the escort *Gruppen* are on the right side after the attack to protect the reassembly of the *Sturmgruppen* without having to change sides. If little or no fighter opposition is encountered, a second attack can be carried out by the *Sturmgruppe*.'

A pilot catches up with his rest on the grass beside Fw 190A-8 'White 5' of II.(*Sturm*)/JG 300 at Holzkirchen in late August 1944. The aircraft is fitted with armoured glass side windscreen panels as well as armoured panels on either side of the cockpit. A parachute is ready on the wing of 'White 10', the next aircraft in line

Leutnant Klaus Neumann had been awarded the Knight's Cross by Hitler in December 1944 for his operations against American heavy bombers. While flying with IV.(*Sturm*)/JG 3, he was accreditated with 17 *Viermots* shot down. In 1945 Neumann flew Me 262s with JG 7 and JV 44

Leutnant Oskar Romm flew with 1./JG 51 over Russia from late 1942 to June 1944, with whom he shot down 76 Soviet aircraft. He was awarded the Knight's Cross on 29 February and transferred to 11.(*Sturm*)/JG 3, before being appointed *Staffelkapitän* of 12.(*Sturm*)/JG 3 on 7 July – a post he held until November, when he became leader of 4./JG 3. After a period with the *Stabsschwarm* of I./EJG 1, Romm returned to command 12.(*Sturm*)/JG 3, before being apointed *Kommandeur* of IV./JG 3 on 17 February 1945, taking over from Major Erwin Bacsila, formerly of *Sturmstaffel* 1. He recorded 92 victories, of which eight were *Viermots* scored while with JG 3. After 283 combat missions, Romm was injured in a crash-landing following combat with Il-2s on 24 April 1945, this incident ending his flying career

In one pass, the combined JG 3/JG 300 attack shot down or 'cut out' 13 B-17s of the 303rd BG near Trier. Dahl claimed two Flying Fortresses, while another bomber fell to Berliner Klaus Bretschneider, who would go on to claim a total of 17 *Viermots*, including three in one day on 7 October, before being shot down and killed by a P-51 while flying against bombers near Kassel on 24 December.

Bretschneider's *Staffel*-mate, Feldwebel Konrad Bauer, also claimed a B-17 for his 13th *Viermot*. 'Pitt' Bauer was a ferocious attack pilot who had shot down three B-24s of the Fifteenth Air Force over Hungary on 27 July 1944. He finally accounted for 14 four-engined bombers out of a total of 39 victories. Bauer, who had been shot down seven times himself and lost two fingers from his right hand while in combat with Mustangs, received the Knight's Cross on 31 October 1944.

Also victorious on 15 August was Oberleutnant Ekkehard Tichy from the Sudetenland and *Kapitän* of 13.*(Sturm)*/JG 3, who shot down a Flying Fortress. Tichy had been wounded in one of his eyes during a clash with escort fighters on 18 March 1944 while with 9./JG 3. He returned to duty, however, having shot down eight *Viermots*, but on 16 August he shot down his 25th, and final, victory – a B-17 – with which he collided, possibly as a result of his impaired vision. Tichy was killed. He was posthumously awarded the Knight's Cross.

Viermot aces continued to emerge, with Feldwebel Willi Reschke of 1./JG 302 knocking down seven bombers in July and six in August, while Unteroffizer Klaus Neumann of 16.*(Sturm)*/JG 3 accounted for eight in August and five in September. On 27 September, the *Staffelkapitän* of 15.*(Sturm)*/JG 3, Leutnant Oskar Romm, shot down three B-24s over Eschwege, while Feldwebel Willi Maximowitz of 14.*(Sturm)*/JG 3 (a *Sturmstaffel* 1 veteran) shot down a pair of B-17s on 2 November. These four pilots alone would account for 62 four-engined bombers by the end of the war.

A report produced by the Eighth Air Force in November 1944 warned;

'It would be a mistake to conclude that the enemy fighter problem has been licked when the average number of bombers lost per month in the first eight months of 1944 was more than twice that for the last eight months of 1943.'

But despite these hard-won successes, time was running out for the Jagdwaffe. From the autumn of 1944, however hard the Germans fought, they were unable to stop the endless maelstrom of Allied air superiority. Allied bombs continued to rain down on the Reich. Paradoxically, the same month as the Eighth Air Force report was published, in an address to the OKL, the *Kommandeur* of I./JG 300, Major Gerhard Stamp, summarised that, 'The problem of the air defence of the Reich is at present not so much a question of how to concentrate our fighter strength but of how to attack effectively the enemy's fighter cover, and thus be able to strike at the bombers, and of how our own fighter losses can, at the same time, be reduced'.

That objective would prove challenging in the months ahead – especially when the RAF joined the USAAF in bombing Germany by day from the autumn of 1944. The first half of December had seen 136 pilots lost in home defence operations, but in the week 23-31 December, German fighter losses on the Western Front were 316 pilots killed or missing.

On 12 December, 140 Lancasters of Bomber Command's No 3 Group attacked the Ruhrstahl steel works at Witten, southwest of Dortmund, escorted by 90 Mustangs of the RAF's No 11 Group. Along with IV./JG 27, I./JG 3 was sent to intercept the British raid and posted claims for 13 Lancasters shot down, including two for Leutnant Franz Ruhl, a long-serving member of 4. *Staffel*. These represented his 36th and 37th victories. Ruhl had shot down his first enemy aircraft in Russia on 10 March 1943 when he claimed an Il-2 destroyed. The second Lancaster on 12 December would be his last confirmed victory, for on Christmas Eve Ruhl's Bf 109G-10 was shot down by US fighters over the Schneeifel and the pilot was killed when it exploded.

But these were eleventh-hour pinpricks for the Allies. Over Christmas in the area of *Luftwaffenkommando West*, the units assigned to the Ardennes offensive reported in excess of 260 casualties. It was a level of attrition that could not be sustained.

In attempting to intercept the American raids against industrial and fuel targets in northern and central Germany on 14 February 1945, the Jagdwaffe lost 107 pilots killed or missing, with another 32 wounded, the heaviest casualties being borne over the Elbe and the Havel by JG 300 and JG 301. Losses amongst the four *Jagdgeschwader* left for Reich defence following a massive transfer of units to the East were rising to nearly 30 per cent of sorties flown, while victories gained amounted to less than 0.2 per cent of Allied strength. With Allied fighters now virtually ruling the skies over Germany, and as a measure of survival, in late February OKL proposed that German fighters should only attack lone bombers straggling behind a formation.

Although the threat posed to Allied bomber formations by the Jagdwaffe had greatly diminished by early 1945, the *jagdflieger* could still, sporadically, hit back – especially with the arrival of a revolutionary new aircraft in frontline service.

Mechanics approach the Fw 190A-8 piloted by Oberleutnant Heinz-Dieter Gramberg of 8./JG 300 as it taxies to a stop at Löbnitz following a mission in early December 1944. A former maritime pilot, Gramberg was based in Italy prior to transferring to the *Sturmgruppe* in late October 1944. He was credited with two victories before being killed by Soviet flak in late January 1945

CHAPTER SEVEN

STORMBIRDS

In the early afternoon of 7 October 1944, in one of the largest daylight bombing raids so far mounted, the Eighth Air Force suffered its first known loss of a heavy bomber to a deadly new form of aircraft when Leutnant Franz Schall, flying a Messerschmitt Me 262 A-1a jet-powered interceptor, attacked B-24s of the 2nd BD during their mission to bomb fuel targets in the Magdeburg area and shot one down. Flying at unprecedented speed, which made him almost impervious to the fighter escort, Schall had used the Me 262's formidable armament of four nose-mounted 30 mm MK 108 cannon to literally blast the Liberator from the air in the Osnabrück area, while his fellow jet pilot, Feldwebel Heinz Lennartz also accounted for one.

It was the moment that USAAF bomber commanders had feared.

Schall was leading three of the new Me 262s of *Kommando Nowotny* up from Hesepe on its first operational sortie. In the autumn of 1944 Adolf Galland had chosen Walter Nowotny, the famed Eastern Front fighter *Experte* and recipient of the Diamonds to the Knight's Cross, to lead a newly formed unit from the concrete runways at Hesepe and Achmer. Using the technological superiority of the Me 262 to full effect, the unit would intercept Allied heavy bombers and their escorts.

Yet Nowotny's pilots, most of them from conventional single-engined fighter units, lacked sufficient training on the new aircraft. This in turn meant that they found the Me 262, with its effortless speed, jet engines, short endurance and rapid descent, difficult to handle. After a shaky start for his *Kommando*, Nowotny himself fell prey to the jet's idiosyncrasies when he was killed in a crash on 7 November 1944 following an attack on bombers.

In many ways, Austrian-born Franz Schall epitomises the pluck and determination of the new jet pilots, and his career would stretch from the embryonic trial missions to the coordinated *Gruppe*-strength operations mounted by JG 7 in

Leutnant Franz Schall, leader of 2./*Kommando Nowotny* (left), stands in front of an Me 262 of the unit, probably at Achmer, in the autumn of 1944. Later appointed *Staffelkapitän* of 10./JG 7, he would see more aerial combat in the Me 262 than most pilots, being credited with the destruction of six *Viermots* while flying the jet

1945. A veteran of the Russian Front with 3./JG 52, he had scored his first victory over an La-5 on 6 May 1943, and by the end of that year had been credited with 26 kills. In 1944 Schall demonstrated a fearsome aptitude for air combat, frequently accounting for multiple victories over Il-2s, U-2s, P-39s and Yak-9s in one day. He was appointed *Staffelkapitän* of 3./JG 52 on 11 August 1944, and by 2 September (the date of his last victory in the East) his tally stood at 116 enemy aircraft destroyed. Schall transferred to jet training with *Kommando Nowotny* on 26 September and was given command of 2. *Staffel*.

Following the award of the Knight's Cross on 10 October and the establishment of JG 7 in November, Schall went on to score 11 jet victories in addition to the six he had achieved with *Kommando Nowotny*, which in addition to the B-24, comprised two B-17s and three Lancasters. He would lead 10./JG 7 until he was killed on 10 April 1945 when, following an emergency landing, his Me 262 struck a bomb crater and exploded.

By January 1945 *Jagdgeschwader* 7 was operating in some strength, with three *Gruppen* of Me 262s defending the airspace around Berlin. Gradually, the unit's ranks were stiffened by the arrival of a small number of experienced *jagdflieger*, including Georg-Peter Eder who began flying the Me 262 with *Erprobungskommando* 262 and *Kommando Nowotny*. He then joined III./JG 7, where he again demonstrated his abilities as an aviator by quickly mastering the Me 262.

It was 'business as usual' for Eder, as leader of 11./JG 7, on 17 January when he claimed a B-17 shot down – this aircraft was probably from the 351st BG, which attacked the Paderborn marshalling yards that day. He had claimed four Boeings shot down (plus three probables) with *Ekdo* 262, followed by five with *Kommando Nowotny*. With the exception of a P-51, all of Eder's seven kills with JG 7 were B-17s. However, he suffered severe injuries when he bailed out of his aircraft after engaging heavy bombers near Bremen on 17 February 1945.

A native of Lüneburg, Leutnant Rudolf Rademacher was a JG 54 veteran who had scored 81 victories flying under Walter Nowotny in Russia prior to serving as a fighter instructor. He had been seriously wounded while flying an Fw 190 in a mission against American heavy bombers on 18 September 1944 and was awarded the Knight's Cross on 30 September for 81 victories in the East. Once he had recovered from his wounds, Rademacher joined 11./JG 7 on 30 January 1945.

On 9 February, the Eighth Air Force bombed northern and central Germany, this time striking at oil, transport and airfield targets including Magdeburg, Lützkendorf and Paderborn. In the Berlin area, a handful of Me 262s from III./JG 7 attacked B-17s, with Rademacher claiming two shot down. He eventually accounted for four Mustangs and an RAF fighter shot down as well, as 11 four-engined bombers, while flying the Me 262.

The *Stabsstaffel* of JG 7 carried out trials using the 21 cm WGr 21 air-to-air mortar fitted to the Me 262 in February. As a makeshift measure, two mortar tubes were mounted on bomb racks beneath the fuselage of some jets, but for how long they were carried and what the results were is not known. What is known is that following the increasingly disappointing results of the mortars fired from piston-engined fighters, German

Leutnant Rudolf Rademacher joined 11./JG 7 with 81 victories to his name, these having been scored over the Eastern Front. He accounted for four P-51s and an RAF fighter shot down while flying the Me 262, as well as 11 four-engined bombers

This Me 262 of 9./JG 7 has been fitted with a 20 kg wooden launch rack, loaded with a dozen 55 mm R4M rockets, on the underside of its starboard wing

armaments experts concluded that the only plausible alternative was for a fighter formation to attack a bomber *Pulk* simultaneously firing batteries of rockets carried either in underwing racks or in nose-mounted 'honeycombs' so that a dense 'fire-chain' could be created which would be impossible for the bombers to avoid.

In June 1944, a requirement was put forward for an electrically fired, fin-stabilised weapon whose warhead would contain sufficient explosive to destroy a four-engined bomber in one hit.

The 55 mm R4M appeared as an 814 mm-long, unrotated, rail or tube-launched, solid fuel-propelled, multi-fin stabilised rocket, with its 520 g warhead contained in an exceptionally thin 1 mm sheet-steel case. With the Me 262, R4Ms were launched from wooden underwing racks that could carry a maximum load of 12 rockets under each wing. It was calculated that the loss of speed incurred to an Me 262 as a result of a launch rack being fitted was approximately 16 km/h.

On 18 March nearly 1200 bombers attacked railway and armaments factories in the Berlin area. They were escorted by 426 fighters. 9./JG 7 put up six aircraft, each fitted with two underwing batteries of 12 of the new R4M rockets. The jets intercepted the *Viermots* over Rathenow, and a total of 144 rockets was fired into the American formation from

In early February 1945, the *Stabsstaffel* of JG 7 carried out trials using the 21 cm WGr 21 air-to-air mortar and, later, 55 mm R4M rockets. Here, two Me 262A-1as of JG 7, seen at either Brandenburg-Briest or Parchim, have been fitted with mortar tubes. The machine in the foreground, 'Green 1', carries a distinctive diagonally striped camouflage scheme, with markings thought to have been those of the *Kommandeur* of III./JG 7, Major Rudolf Sinner.

distances of between 400-600 metres. Pilots reported astonishing amounts of resulting debris and aluminium fragments – pieces of wing, engines and cockpits flying through the air from aircraft hit by the weapons.

Oberfähnrich Walter Windisch, who had joined the Luftwaffe in 1943 and who had two victories to his credit by the time he was transferred to JG 7 from JG 52, was one of the first pilots of the *Geschwader* to see the effects of the R4M on enemy bombers;

'I was on that first sortie during which R4M rockets were used, and I experienced something beyond my comprehension. The destructive effect against the targets was immense. It almost gave me a feeling of being invincible. However, the launching grids for the rockets were not of optimum design – they were still too rough and ready and, compared with conventionally-powered aircraft, when you went into a turn with the Me 262, flying became a lot more difficult because the trimming was not too good.'

Windisch would go on to claim five four-engined bombers shot down while with JG 7, the first on 15 March when he accounted for a B-24 during an attack against the German military headquarters at Zossen. Leutnant Erich Müller claimed two bombers in the same mission, while Oberfähnrich Pfeiffer shot down another. Rudolf Rademacher accounted for a bomber, while Leutnant Karl Schnörrer claimed two.

Schnörrer, a native of Nürnberg, had served with I./JG 54 and claimed his first victory over the Eastern Front in December 1941. In late 1942, Walter Nowotny had selected Schnörrer to fly as his wingman, and the two men became close friends. Despite a reputation for being a hard man on his aircraft following three landing accidents whilst at the controls of Bf 109s, Schnörrer became an invaluable and trusted partner to Nowotny during the latter's stellar rise as a fighter ace. It is perhaps a measure of his priorities that Schnörrer, who had earned himself the somewhat unjust nickname of *'Quax'* after an accident-prone cartoon character, had scored just 20 victories by 18 August 1943, against his flight leader's tally of 151.

On 12 November 1943 Schnörrer engaged a formation of Il-2s and shot one down for his 35th victory, but in doing so was badly wounded, forced to bail out and subsequently injured both legs. Having recovered by mid-1944, he transferred with Nowotny to his new jet *Kommando* and proceeded onto JG 7. Of his 11 victories flying the Me 262, nine were B-17s, including two downed on one day on 18 and 30 March 1945. On this latter date, Schnörrer engaged Flying Fortresses over Lüneberg, but as he pulled away from the scene of combat, his jet was hit by defensive fire from the bomber formation. Turning for home, he was chased by P-51s, and decided the best course of action would be to bail out. In doing so, he struck the tail unit of his jet and – once again – badly injured his legs. Despite this, he managed to land by parachute, but his flying days were over.

As the war entered its final weeks and defeat loomed for the Third Reich, the pilots of JG 7 fought on regardless.

The last day of March 1945 would see another major effort in the relentless Allied bombing offensive. While the Eighth Air Force struck at oil refineries in northern and central Germany, RAF Bomber Command aimed for the Blohm and Voss shipyards in Hamburg. A force of

On 30 March 1945, Leutnant Karl Schnörrer, commander of 11./JG 7 and former wingman to Walter Nowotny, was chased by P-51s following an engagement against American bombers over northwest Germany during which he shot down two B-17s. These proved to be his last victories of the war for he was forced to bail out a short while later, injuring his legs for a second time

CHAPTER SEVEN

469 Lancasters, Halifaxes and Mosquitoes arrived over a cloud-covered target, but still bombed, inflicting considerable damage to the southern districts of the port city. Against this raid, 2. *Jagddivision* deployed some 20 jets from I. and III./JG 7 that intercepted Lancasters as they approached Bremen.

On this occasion, fortune was to favour the defenders as, in addition to 30 mm cannon shells, repeated salvos of R4M missiles streaked into the British formation. For the crews of the Lancasters, the German skies became a scene of smoke-blackened carnage as bombers exploded and shattered wings and engines spun away from fuselages. Oberfeldwebel Hermann Buchner of 9./JG 7 recalled what happened after the rockets had been fired;

'I made a right turn and lined up for another attack. This was made using the nose cannon. My Lancaster lay directly in my sights, and I only had to get a bit closer. Now, I opened fire, the hits were good, but the pilot of the Lancaster must have been an old hand. He turned his bomber steeply over on its right wing, making a tight turn around the main axis. With my speed, I was unable to see if my shots had had any effect, or to see how he flew on. I had to think about returning home. We had a shortage of fuel in the Me 262. The other pilots were also having the same problem.'

Nevertheless, Oberleutnant Hans 'Specker' Grünberg, *Staffelkapitän* of 1./JG 7, shot down two Lancasters in the action over Hamburg, as did Leutnant Gustav Sturm of 9. *Staffel*.

Grünberg is credited with 82 victories scored in 550 missions, including the destruction of seven Il-2s in three sorties in Russia in July 1943 whilst with 5./JG 3. He was awarded the Knight's Cross in July 1944. All of his five jet victories were *Viermots*, with another six scored flying the Bf 109.

Gustav Sturm's first victory was a B-24 shot down over North Africa on 15 November 1942 while flying with 2./JG 27. Without exception, his next 11 kills were four-engined bombers scored over Germany or Austria between August 1943 and May 1944. Sturm served briefly with

Me 262A-1a 'Green 3' of the *Geschwaderstab* of JG 7 prepares to move off across the concrete surface at Brandenburg-Briest in February or early March 1945. The aircraft, finished in a relatively rare application of streaked horizontal lines, has been fitted with a pair of 21 cm WGr air-to-air mortar tubes visible beneath the fuselage aft of the nosewheel

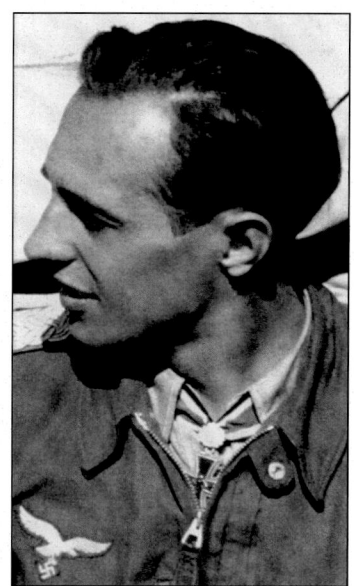

Major Erich Rudorffer, photographed in the West in 1942 while commanding 6./JG 2. In the final months of the war this 136-victory ace and recipient of the Knight's Cross with Oakleaves and Swords, took command of I./JG 7. He personally accounted for ten four-engined bombers destroyed, all scored while flying the Me 262

6./JG 3 and JG 51, before transferring to III./JG 7 in March 1945. On 25 April 1945 – the day JG 7 flew what was probably its last operation against American bombers, when 276 B-17s of the Eighth Air Force attacked Pilsen, in Czechoslovakia – Sturm, based with his *Staffel* at Prague, attempted to rescue a comrade from the flaming confines of his cockpit following a crash-landing. However, as he reached the burning jet, it exploded, and Sturm suffered severe chest injuries. He was credited with 22 victories, including 11 *Viermots*.

During April 1945 seven B-17s went down to the guns of Major Erich Rudorffer, a 136-victory ace and recipient of the Knight's Cross with Oakleaves and Swords who led I./JG 7.

Flying since the French campaign of May 1940, during which he was an NCO pilot with JG 2, Rudorffer was awarded the Knight's Cross a year later for his 19 victories. He proved to be a potent adversary against the Western Allies, shooting down two Spitfires in one day over Dieppe in August 1942. In November of that year Rudorffer was appointed *Staffelkapitän* of 6./JG 2 and his unit moved to Tunisia, where he shot down eight British aircraft in 32 minutes on 9 February 1943. Six days later, in a remarkable feat, seven more enemy aircraft fell to his guns. Rudorffer subsequently took command of II./JG 2, but returned to France in April 1943.

By the time he left the *Richthofen Geschwader* to take up his appointment as *Kommandeur* of the new IV./JG 54 in June, Rudorffer had accumulated 74 victories. Just weeks later, however, he was transferred to the East to take over II./JG 54 following the loss of that *Gruppe's* previous commander. Over Russia, Rudorffer excelled himself, and on one occasion claimed 13 Soviet machines shot down in 17 minutes. The Oakleaves to the Knight's Cross followed on 11 April 1944 when his tally stood at 134 victories. There followed several more incidents of multiple kills in one day over the Eastern Front before Rudorffer was awarded the Swords to Knight's Cross upon his 212th victory on 26 January 1945 – he was the 126th such recipient.

Rudorffer would end the war having clocked up more than 1000 missions, during which he had encountered the enemy more than 300 times. He had also bailed out on no fewer than nine occasions and been shot down 16 times. Rudorffer accounted for ten four-engined bombers destroyed, all while flying the Me 262.

Perhaps Johannes Steinhoff, the former *Kommodore* of JG 77, JG 7 and a member of JV 44, best summarised the ill-fated combat debut of the Me 262 in the final months of the war in Europe during a talk in the late 1960s;

'Even if all available jet fighters had been deployed for attacks on bombers, I do not believe that the fortunes of war would have changed for us.

'The survivors who took part in those great aerial battles against the bombers agree with me that attacking those Flying Fortresses and Liberators was not a pleasure. Those who, like myself, flew those attacks and manoeuvred through the stream of innumerable bombers will never be able to forget that picture, and I am sure that there is not one who would claim that he did not feel relieved when he had landed back home in one piece.'

APPENDICES

APPENDIX 1

Single-engined fighter aces with 20 or more *Viermot* victories

Meaningful analysis of this list in order to establish which pilots, on average, achieved the shortest time-to-kills ratios, and thus who were the most effective, is virtually impossible. Variable criteria such as the level of Allied bombing activity in any given area or theatre at any given time, the date of death of the pilot in action, weather and operating factors such as the weight of enemy escort, come into play. I would like to acknowledge the data contained at www.luftwaffe.cz in the preparation of this list.

	Total victories	Known four-engined Victories	Period in which four-engined victories scored
Major Georg-Peter Eder	78	36	Dec 1942–Feb 1945
Major Anton Hackl	192	34	Jun 1943–Dec 1944?
Oberleutnant Konrad Bauer	57	32	Apr 1944–Aug 1944
Oberstleutnant Walter Dahl	126	30	Sept 1943–Jan 1945?
Major Rolf-Günther Hermichen	64	26	Jul 1943–Mar 1944
Oberstleutnant Egon Mayer	102	26	Nov 1942–Jan 1944 (KIA Mar 1944)
Leutnant Anton-Rudolf Piffer	35	26	May 1943–May 1944 (KIA Jun 1944)
Major Werner Schroer	114	26	Dec 1942–May 1944
Major Hermann Staiger	63	26	Jul 1943–Dec 1944
Leutnant Alwin Doppler	29	25	?
Hauptmann Hugo Frey	32	25	Jan 1943–Mar 1944 (KIA Mar 1944)
Oberstleutnant Kurt Bühligen	112	24	?
Hauptmann Hans Ehlers	55	24	Dec 1942–Dec 1944 (KIA Dec 1944)
Oberfeldwebel Walter Loos	38	22	Mar 1944–Aug 1944
Major Friedrich-Karl Müller	140	23	Jan 1943–May 1944 (Killed May 1944)
Hauptmann Hans Weik	36	22	Sept 1943–Jul 1944
Hauptmann Heinrich Wurzer	26	23	Nov 1943–July 1944 (2 night)
Oberleutnant Werner Gerth	27	22	Feb 1944–Nov 1944 (KIA Nov 1944)
Oberstleutnant Heinz Bär	221	21	?
Hauptmann Fritz Karch	47	21	?
Leutnant Willi Unger	24	21	Apr 1944–Oct 1944
Oberleutnant Wilhelm Kientsch	53	20	Apr 1943–Dec 1943 (KIA Jan 1944)
Hauptmann Hans-Heinrich Koenig	28	20	Oct 1943–May 1944 (KIA May 1944)
Oberfeldwebel Wille Reschke	27	20	Jul 1944–Jan 1945
Hauptmann Josef Wurmheller	102	20+	Feb 1943–April 1944 (KIA Jun 1944)

Number of pilots with 19 confirmed four-engined victories = 4
Number of pilots with 18 confirmed four-engined victories = 4
Number of pilots with 17 confirmed four-engined victories = 5
Number of pilots with 16 confirmed four-engined victories = 3
Number of pilots with 15 confirmed four-engined victories = 7
Number of pilots with 14 confirmed four-engined victories = 7
Number of pilots with 13 confirmed four-engined victories = 8
Number of pilots with 12 confirmed four-engined victories = 12
Number of pilots with 11 confirmed four-engined victories = 9
Number of pilots with 10 confirmed four-engined victories = 24

Zerstörer Aces with 10 or more *Viermot* victories in total

Leutnant Rudolf Dassow   12 four-engined victories
Hauptmann Peter Jenne   12
Hauptmann Herbert Schob   10

APPENDIX 2

Facsimile diagrams showing 'Evolution of Relative Firepower of Fw 190 versus B-17' (right) and 'One USAAF four-engined bomber versus one Me 110 with 21 cm RPs' (below) taken from the United States Strategic Bombing Survey *The Defeat of the German Air Force*, published by the Military Analysis Division in October 1945.

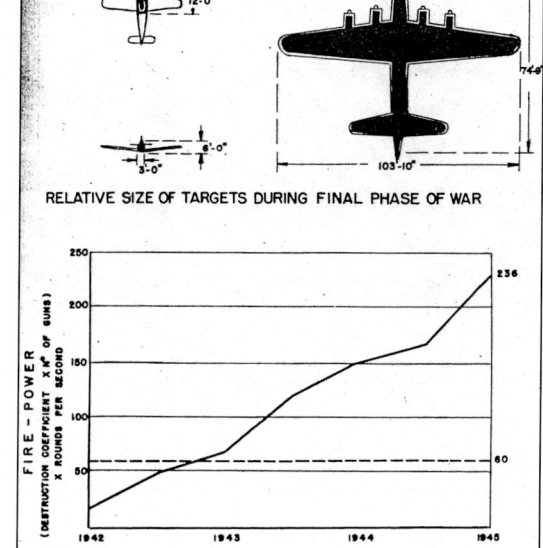

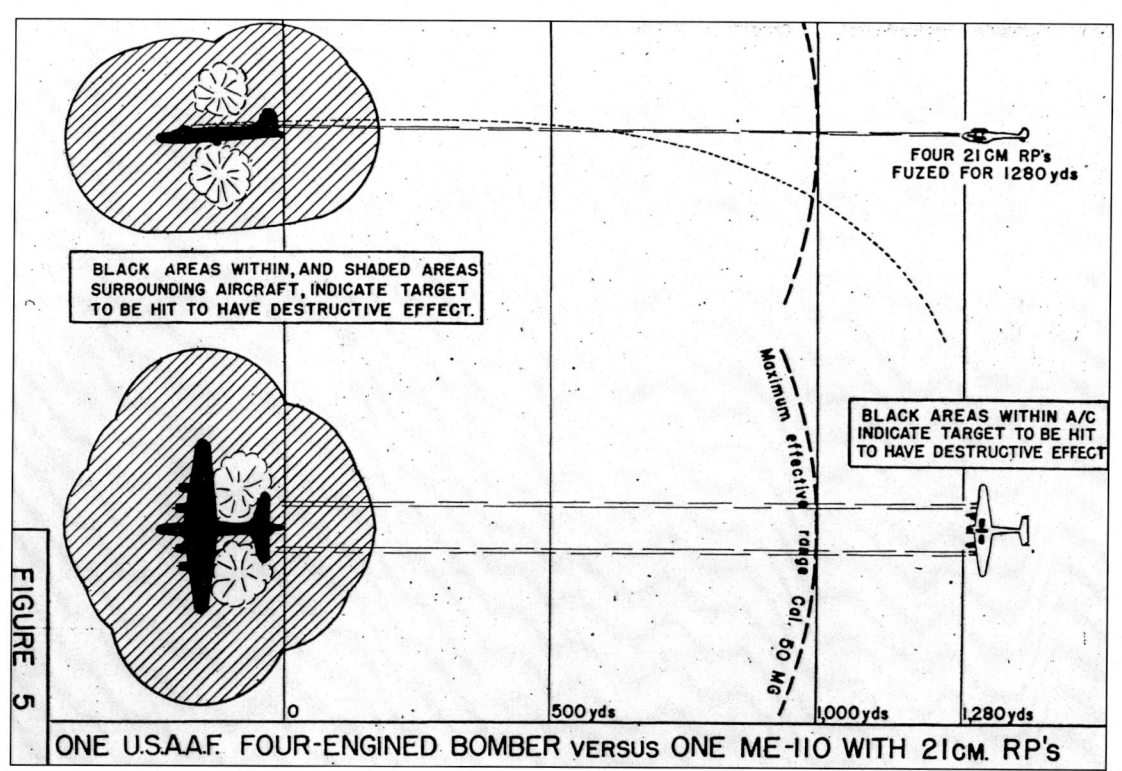

Colour Plates

1
Bf 109F-4 'Black Chevron and Bars' of Major Walter Oesau, *Geschwaderkommodore* JG 2, Beaumont le Roger, France, April 1942

One of two Bf 109Fs believed to have been flown by Oesau in 1942, this aircraft had yellow applied to its cowling underside and rudder. Its spinner was probably in *Schwarzgrün*. The aircraft may have also carried the red scripted 'R' of the *Richthofen Geschwader*, although there is no photographic evidence to prove this conclusively.

2
Fw 190A-4 'Double White Chevron' of Hauptmann Egon Mayer, *Gruppenkommandeur* III./JG 2, Brittany, France, late 1942/early 1943

Mayer's aircraft carries the distinctive cockerel's head emblem of III./JG 2, as well as 62 victory markings on a yellow rudder. Six of these denote his success against USAAF four-engined bombers between November 1942 and January 1943.

3
Fw 190A-6 'Brown 1' of Hauptmann Johannes Naumann, *Staffelkapitän* 6./JG 26, Lille-Vendeville, France, July 1943

Seen in typical finish for JG 26 Fw 190s in the West at this time, 'Brown 1' had its port-side undercarriage door removed for a short period of time. This was possibly in preparation for the fitting of a centreline drop tank.

4
Bf 109G-6 Wk-Nr. 18 216 'Black 10' of Feldwebel Hans-Gerd Wennekers, 5./JG 11, Mönchen-Gladbach, Germany, June 1943

Wenneker's Messerschmitt had a yellow underside to its cowling, a red fuselage identification band and three victory markings on its rudder. The latter represented a Liberator and two Flying Fortresses credited to the pilot between February and May 1943.

5
Bf 109G-6 'White 10' of Leutnant Franz Ruhl, *Staffelkapitän* 4./JG 3, Schiphol, Holland, winter 1943/44

Ruhl's machine had a fairly worn appearance, especially along the top of the fuselage just aft of the canopy. A small red circle (originally adopted in Russia) was applied immediately below the JG 3 emblem in order to give the latter the vague appearance of an exclamation mark.

6
Bf 109G-6 'White 10' of Oberleutnant Alfred Grislawski, 1./JG 50, Wiesbaden-Erbenheim, Germany, late September 1943

Grislawski's colourfully marked Bf 109 had a yellow cowling underside and the emblem of JG 50 beneath the cockpit. The white rudder carried a rendition of the Knight's Cross, the pilot's monogrammed initials and 112 victory markings, the last three of which were B-17s claimed on 17 August and 6 September 1943.

7
Bf 109G-6 Wk-Nr. 18 105 'Black 12' of Unteroffiziere Karl-Heinz Böttner and Helmut Schwarzenhölzer, 8./JG 77, Chilivani, Sicily, July 1943

Typical of the aircraft used by JG 77 in the battle against *Viermots* over Sicily, this Bf 109 carried the unit's *'Herz-As'* (Ace of Hearts) emblem and its unusually sized and located aircraft code numbers. The emblem forward of the aircraft number is that of III./JG 77, outlined with the titling *'Wander-Zirkus Ubben'* (the 'Ubben Travelling Circus') inspired by the then *Kapitän* of 8. *Staffel*, and subsequent *Kommandeur* of III. *Gruppe*, Major Kurt Ubben.

8
Bf 109G-6 'Double Black Chevron' of Hauptmann Karl Rammelt, *Gruppenkommandeur* II./JG 51, Udine, Italy, December 1943

Rammelt's aircraft was adorned with the JG 51 *Geschwader* emblem as well as a personal marking in the form of a spiked mace beneath the cockpit, aft of which was the unusually positioned *Gruppe* bar. The rear fuselage also bore the white Mediterranean Theatre band. The rudder was marked with 34 victory bars, recording Rammelt's kills up to the end of 1943.

9 and 10
Fw 190A-6 'Double Chevron' of Major Anton Hackl, *Geschwaderkommodore*, JG 11, Oldenburg, Germany, April 1944

Hackl's Focke-Wulf carries the emblem of the *Stab* of III. *Gruppe* (of which he had recently been *Kommandeur*), together with *Stab* markings, yellow unit identification band and a white rudder. The latter has been adorned with a rendition of the Knight's Cross encased in oak leaves showing a total of 141 victories, his last kill being a B-24 shot down over Lingen on 11 April 1944.

11
Fw 190A-7 Wk-Nr. 430172 'Black 1' of Leutnant Rudiger Kirchmayr, *Staffelkapitän* 5./JG 1, Rheine, Germany, January 1944

One of several machines known to have been flown by Kirchmayr, this aircraft is very representative of II. *Gruppe* Fw 190s of the time. It had the winged '1' *Geschwader* emblem applied in the usual nose position, as well as the red *Geschwader* fuselage band.

12
Fw 190A-8 WNr. 680143 'White 9' of Gefreiter Walter Gehr, 4./JG 1, Störmede, Germany, May 1944

The aircraft is in a standard scheme, although it lacks the *Geschwader* emblem. Gefreiter Gehr recorded his first victory in this aircraft when he shot down a B-24 west of Magdeburg at 1407 hrs on 28 May 1944. He expended 230 rounds of MG 131 and MG 151 ammunition in the process.

13
Fw 190A-7 'Yellow 5' of 6./JG 1, Störmede, Germany, May 1944

This aircraft also has the winged '1' *Geschwader* emblem on its cowling and the red unit identification band of JG 1, as well as the II. *Gruppe* bar and a standard scheme for fighter aircraft deployed in the defence of the Reich at this time.

14
Fw 190A-7 'Red 22' of Oberfeldwebel Leo Schuhmacher, *Gruppenstab* II./JG 1, Störmede, Germany, April 1944

Heinz Bär's wingman claimed his 13th victory in this aircraft when he shot down a B-17F north of Fallersleben on 11 April 1944 using 80 rounds of MG 131 and 80 rounds of MG 151 ammunition. 'Red 22' has veen marked with the winged '1' *Geschwader* emblem and the red unit identification band assigned to JG 1.

15
Bf 110G-2 3U+KR of 7./ZG 26, Königsberg-Neumark, Germany, late 1943/early 1944

Possibly the aircraft of Hauptmann Johannes Kiel, *Staffelkapitän* of 7./ZG 26 and later *Gruppenkommandeur* of II. *Gruppe*, this Bf 110 still carries its white Mediterranean theatre markings. It is fitted with twin underwing 21 cm WGr mortar tubes.

16
Bf 110G-2/R3 2N+EM of 4./ZG 76, Königsberg-Neumark, Germany, early 1944

This Bf 110 of Hauptmann Helmut Haugk's 4. *Staffel* is finished in a generally clean standard grey scheme with yellow fuselage band, white aircraft letter and red/white spinner tips. The aircraft carries twin underwing 21 cm WGr mortar tubes and a MG 151 weapons pack beneath the central fuselage for anti-bomber work.

17
Me 210A-0(1) Wk-Nr. 2100110049 2N+FR of 7./ZG 1, Wels, Austria, early 1944

This Me 210 was finished in a dark grey standard late-war scheme with toned down *Balkenkreuz* and fuselage code letters. The aircraft was fitted with twin underwing 21 cm WGr mortar tubes.

18
Me 410A-1/U4 Wk-Nr. 420481 3U+LP of 6./ZG 26, Königsberg-Neumark, Germany, April 1944

This BK 5 cm cannon-equipped aircraft was finished in a standard late-war grey mottle with a white fuselage band and the *Gruppe* clog emblem applied to the outer panelling of both engines. The three-digit numeral painted high on the tail assembly may have been a part and/or transit number.

19
Me 410A-1/U4 Wk-Nr. 420292 3U+CC of *Stab* II./ZG 26, Königsberg-Neumark, Germany, May 1944

In addition to the prominent 5 cm BK 5 in the nose, this aircraft was fitted with 37 mm cannon on the bomb-bays for anti-bomber operations. Its individual letter is in the *Stab* colour of green and the machine has a white fuselage band, possibly a legacy from the Mediterranean Theatre. The *Gruppe's* yellow clog emblem was applied to the outer panelling of both engines.

20
Bf 109G-2 'Yellow 6' of Feldwebel Albert Palm, 3./JG 4, Mizil, Rumania, August 1943

Palm had previously served 8./JG 77, and at the time of leaving that *Staffel* to join 3./JG 4 he had 28 victories to his credit. This aircraft bears the personal incription '*Mäuschen*' ('Little Mouse') beneath the cockpit, and it also has the distinctive American-style fuselage numeral found on a number of I. *Gruppe* Bf 109s. The fighter also boasts a yellow Theatre band. Yellow was applied to the tip of the spinner as well, whilst the rest of it was segmented in black/green and white.

21
Bf 109G-6 'White 17' of 7./JG 53, Villaorba, Italy, December 1943

This aircraft is typical of the Bf 109s of JG 53 that were in action against USAAF bombers over the southern Mediterranean in late 1943. The spinner was segmented in black/green and white. The '*Pik-As*' ('Ace of Spades') emblem of JG 53 is carried in the usual position on the nose and the aircraft has a white Theatre fuselage band. The aircraft also carries a drop tank for extended range over water as well as 21 cm WGr mortar tubes.

22
Bf 109G-6 'White 8' of I./JG 27, Fels am Wagram, Austria, early 1944

In addition to its green unit fuselage identification band, this machine's white rudder may denote that was assigned to a *Staffelkapitän* or *Staffelführer*. The *Gruppe* emblem was applied to both sides of the cowling, with the head of the lioness facing forward. The aircraft is fitted with underwing gondolas for 20 mm MG 151 cannon.

23
Fw 190A-7 Wk-Nr. 642559 'White 3' of Unteroffiziere Erich Lambertus and Gerhard Vivroux, *Sturmstaffel* 1, Salzwedel, Germany, February 1944

Like many of the Fw 190s of *Sturmstaffel* 1, this aircraft has been fitted with armoured '*Panzerglas*' front and side canopy panels and also the armoured side panels to the cockpit walls for protection when making close-range attacks on enemy bombers. The aircraft has the black-white-black fuselage band of the *Staffel*.

24
Fw 190A-8/R2 'Yellow 17' of Unteroffizier Willi Unger, 12./JG 3, Barth, May 1944

This aircraft is finished in a typical late-war mottle and has a white fuselage band applied that has in turn been adorned with the black wavy bar of IV. *Gruppe*. The fighter is fitted with wing-mounted 20 mm MG 151 and 30 mm MK 108 cannon, but the installations for two 13 mm machine guns in the upper cowling above the engine have been faired over. It is also fitted with additional cockpit armour and carries a WGr 21 '*Krebsgerät*' rearward-firing 21cm mortar tube beneath its fuselage. Intended to be fired 'back' at a bomber formation following a firing pass, this weapon achieved mixed results as it adversely affected the Focke-Wulf's speed and manoeuvrability.

25
Fw 190A-8/R2 'Double Chevron' of Hauptmann Wilhelm Moritz, Stab IV.(Sturm)/JG 3, Memmingen, Germany, July 1944

This aircraft was photographed outside a hangar following a mission on 18 July 1944, and was distinctly different from the one usually associated with Moritz in that it had a white fuselage band applied, over which had been painted a black wavy *Gruppe* line. The aircraft had a dark grey or all-black forward cowling, aft of which was a stylised eagle's wing and armoured glass cockpit panels and cockpit side armour.

26
Fw 190A-8/R2 'Black 13' of Lt Werner Gerth, 11.(Sturm)/JG 3, Memmingen, Germany, July 1944

Gerth's aircraft bore a slightly darker than usual field-mixed finish, and a stylised eagle's wing was applied to the fuselage aft of an all-black forward cowling, upon which was applied the emblem of JG 3 *'Udet'*. The rear fuselage carried the white unit identification band and *Gruppe* marking.

27
Fw 190A-8 'Blue 14' of Feldwebel Walter Loos, Stab/JG 300, Bad Worishofen, Germany, August 1944

Loos' Fw 190 was finished in a typically late-war mottled scheme, with the tactical number in bright blue outlined in white, along with a red JG 300 fuselage identification band.

28
Fw 190A-8 Wk-Nr. 171641 'Red 3' of Feldwebel Konrad 'Pitt' Bauer, 5./JG 300, Erfurt-Bindersleben, Germany, August 1944

Bauer's aircraft was finished in a pale mottle, with no fuselage band. The small yellow circle on the upper cowling panel indicates the fitting of an engine power-boost system. The pilot's motto beneath the cockpit reads *'Kornjark'*.

29
Me 262A-1a 'Green 4' of Major Theodor Weissenberger, Geschwaderstab JG 7, Brandenburg-Briest, Germany, February-March 1945

This jet features extended horizontal bars in black, outlined in white, denoting its assignment to the *Kommodore*. The upper third of light blue on the *Geschwader's* running fox emblem is unusually large, suggesting that the whole emblem has been partially applied over another one.

30
Me 262A-1a Wk-.Nr. 110800 'White 7' of Unteroffizier Günther Engler, 3./JG 7, Brandenburg-Briest, Germany, February 1945

This aircraft features the running fox emblem of JG 7 in the commonly seen location on the nose, while the *Hakenkreuz* on the tail is in solid white – quite common feature on many of JG 7's aircraft. It would appear that the aircraft also carried the blue and red Reich air defence fuselage identification band. The fighter has been fitted with R4M rockets.

31
Me 262A-1a 'Green 3', Geschwaderstab JG 7, Brandenburg-Briest, Germany, February-March 1945

The fighter's tactical number 'Green 3' is quite unusual in style, and there appear to be no other markings, nor a defence of the Reich fuselage band on what is probably a very typical JG 7 machine engaged in the defence of the Germany. The rudder is lighter in colour, suggesting a replacement part.

BIBLIOGRAPHY

Non-published material

Miscellaneous

Headquarters USAFE: *Air Staff Post Hostilities Intelligence Requirements on the German Air Force – Tactical Employment (Section IV C): Fighter Operations*, 10 December 1945 (IWM, London)
(including)
Appendix XVI *A History of the German Air Force Twin-Engine Fighter Arm (Zerstörerwaffe)* by Galland, Kowalewski, Nolle and Eschenauer, 8 October 1945
Appendix XXXI *Conduct of a Company Front Attack*, Dahl, 20 September 1945
Appendix XXXII *Conduct of a Mission in the Defense of the Reich*, Dahl, 20 September 1945
The Birth, Life and Death of the German Day Fighter Arm (related by Adolf Galland), ADI(K) Report No. 373/1945 (Pegg)
Headquarters, Eighth Air Force, Operational Analysis Section: *An Evaluation of Defensive Measures Taken to Protect Heavy Bombers from Loss and Damage since the Beginning of Operations in the European Theater*, November 1944 (Nijboer)
German Fighter Tactics against RAF Day Bombers, Air Ministry Weekly Intelligence Summary, 3 March 1945 (Smith)
Willi Unger, *15.Sturm/Jagdgeschwader Udet – Abschußmeldung, 7.7.44* (Unger)

Bundesarchiv-Militärarchiv, Freiburg

RL 10/403 *Abschussmeldung* and *Frontfilmauswertung* (*Sturmstaffel* 1)
RL10/433 Miscellaneous *Abschussmeldung* (II./JG 1)

UK National Archives, Kew

AIR2/7493 – *Tactical Notes on the Operations of the Fortresses (B-17F) of the USAAF in the European Theatre of War up to September 15th, 1942*
AIR20/8534 – *German Fighter Tactics against RAF Bomber Formations in Africa*, CSDIC (Air), CMF, Report No. 597, 23rd October 1945
AIR22/78 – Air Ministry Weekly Intelligence Summaries 187-212, Apr-Sept 1943
AIR40/358 – *Eighth Air Force Narrative of Operations 298th Operation – 11 April 1944*
AIR40/371 – *Composite Intelligence Narrative No. 9 of Operations undertaken 23 November 1942* by USAAF and RAF, HQ Eighth Air Force, Widewing, 26 November 1942
AIR40/463 – *Synopsis Report, 114th Operation – Mission No 1 – 3rd Bomb Division*, VIII Bomber Command, 11 October 1943
AIR40/598 – VIII Bomber Command: *Operation 298: aircraft factories and industrial targets Germany and Poland, 11 Apr 1944*

AIR40/613 – VIII Bomber Command: *Operation 327: Berlin, Magdeburg and Brandenburg, 29 Apr 1944*

Articles

BUCHLING, NILS, *Operational use of the 50 mm Cannon by II./ZG 26 'Horst Wessel' in the Defense of the Reich 1944*, Luftwaffe im Focus, Edition No 17, Luftfahrtverlag Start, Bad Zwischenahn, 2010

STEINHOFF, Lt Gen JOHANNES (transl. and ed. Lt Col William Geffen), *The German Battle against the American Bombers* in *'Command & Commanders in Modern Military History'*, Proceedings of the Second Military History Symposium, USAF Academy, 1968

Books

BERGSTROM, CHRISTER, ANTIPOV, VLAD and SUNDIN, CLAES, *Graf & Grislawski – A Pair of Aces*, Eagle Editions, Hamilton, 2003

CALDWELL, DONALD, *JG 26 – Top Guns of the Luftwaffe*, Orion Books, New York, 1991

CALDWELL, DONALD, *The JG 26 War Diary Volume One 1939-1942*, Grub Street, London, 1996

CALDWELL, DONALD, *The JG 26 War Diary Volume Two 1943-1945*, Grub Street, London, 1998

CALDWELL, DONALD and MULLER, RICHARD, *The Luftwaffe over Germany – Defense of the Reich*, Greenhill Books, London, 2007

CRAVEN, W F and CATE, J L, *The Army Air Forces in World War II, Volume I – Plans and Early Operations (January 1939 to August 1942)*, University of Chicago Press, Chicago, 1948

DIERICH, WOLFGANG, *Die Verbände der Luftwaffe 1935-1945*, Verlag Heinz Nickel, Zweibrücken, 1993

ENGAU, FRITZ, *Frontal durch die Bomberpulks*, Winkler, Lassnitzhöhe, 1997

ETHELL, JEFFREY and PRICE, ALFRED, *Target Berlin – Mission 250: 6 March 1944*, Jane's Publishing, London, 1981

FORSYTH, ROBERT, *Jagdwaffe – Defending the Reich 1943-1944*, Classic Publications, Hersham, 2004

FORSYTH, ROBERT, *Jagdwaffe – Defending the Reich 1944-1945*, Classic Publications, Hersham, 2005

FREEMAN, ROGER, *The US Strategic Bomber*, Macdonald and Jane's, London, 1975

FREEMAN, ROGER A, *Mighty Eighth War Diary*, Janes, London, 1981

FREEMAN, ROGER A, *Mighty Eighth War Manual*, Janes, London, 1984

HAMMEL, ERIC, *Air War Europa – America's Air War against Germany in Europe and North Africa: Chronology 1942-1945*, Pacifica Press, Pacifica, 1994

HAMMEL, ERIC, *The Road to Big Week – The Struggle for Daylight Air Supremacy over Western Europe July 1942-February 1944*, Pacifica Military History, Pacifica, 2009

HESS, WILLIAM, *Combat Aircraft 38 – B-17 Flying Fortress Units of the MTO*, Osprey Publishing, Oxford, 2003

HOOTON, E R, *The Luftwaffe – A Study in Air Power 1933-1945*, Classic Publications, Hersham, 2010

IRVING, DAVID, *Churchill's War Volume II, Triumph in Adversity*, Focal Point Publications, London, 2001

LORANT, JEAN-YVES and GOYAT, RICHARD, *Jagdgeschwader 300 'Wilde Sau' Volume One – June 1943-September 1944*, Eagle Editions, Hamilton, 2005

LORANT, JEAN-YVES and GOYAT, RICHARD, *Jagdgeschwader 300 'Wilde Sau' Volume Two – September 1944-May 1945*, Eagle Editions, Hamilton, 2007

MIDDLEBROOK, MARTIN and EVERITT, CHRIS, *The Bomber Command War Diaries – An Operational Reference Book 1939-1945*, Penguin Books, London, 1990

Target: Germany – The US Army Air Forces' official story of the VIII Bomber Command's first year over Europe, HMSO, London, 1944

MOMBEEK, ERIC with FORSYTH, ROBERT and CREEK, EDDIE J, *Sturmstaffel 1 – Reich Defence 1943-1944 The War Diary*, Classic Publications, Crowborough, 1999

MOMBEEK, ERIC, *Defenders of the Reich – Jagdgeschwader 1 Volume One 1942*, Classic Publications, Hersham, 2001

MOMBEEK, ERIC, *Defenders of the Reich – Jagdgeschwader 1 Volume Two 1943*, Classic Publications, Hersham, 2001

OBERMAIER, ERNST, *Die Ritterkreuzträger der Luftwaffe 1939-1945 – Band I Jagdflieger*, Verlag Dieter Hoffmann, Mainz, 1966 and 1982

PRIEN, JOCHEN and RODEIKE, PETER, *Jagdgeschwader 1 und 11 Teil 1 1939-1943*, Struve-Druck, Eutin, undated

PRIEN, JOCHEN and RODEIKE, PETER, *Jagdgeschwader 1 und 11 Teil 2 1944*, Struve-Druck, Eutin, undated

PRIEN, JOCHEN, and RODEIKE, PETER, *Jagdgeschwader 1 und 11 Teil 3 1944-1945*, Struve-Druck, Eutin, undated

PRIEN, JOCHEN and STEMMER, GERHARD, *Messerschmitt Bf 109 im Einsatz bei der II./Jagdgeschwader 3*, Struve-Druck, Eutin, undated

PRIEN, JOCHEN, *IV./Jagdgeschwader 3 – Chronik einer Jagdgruppe 1943-1945*, Struve-Druck, Eutin, undated

PRIEN, JOCHEN, RODEIKE, PETER and STEMMER, GERHARD *Messerschmitt Bf 109 im Einsatz bei Stab und I./Jagdgeschwader 27*, Struve-Druck, Eutin, undated

PRIEN, JOCHEN, RODEIKE, PETER and STEMMER, GERHARD, *Messerschmitt Bf 109 im Einsatz bei der II./Jagdgeschwader 27*, Struve-Druck, Eutin, undated

PRIEN, JOCHEN, *'Pik-As' Geschichte des Jagdgeschwaders 53, Teil 3*, Hamburg, 1991

PRIEN, JOCHEN, *Geschichte des Jagdgeschwaders 77, Teil 3 1942-1943*, Struve-Druck, Eutin, undated

PRIEN, JOCHEN, *Geschichte des Jagdgeschwaders 77, Teil 4 1944-1945*, Struve-Druck, Eutin, undated

RESCHKE, WILLI, *Jagdgeschwader 301/302 'Wilde Sau'*, Motorbuch Verlag, Stuttgart, 1998

SMITH, J RICHARD and CREEK, EDDIE J, *Me 262 Volume Two*, Classic Publications, Burgess Hill, 1998

TERRAINE, JOHN, *The Right of the Line – The Royal Air Force in the European War 1939-1945*, Hodder and Stoughton, London, 1985

WEAL, JOHN, *Aviation Elite Units 1 – Jagdgeschwader 2 'Richthofen'*, Osprey Publishing, Botley, 2000

WEAL, JOHN *Aircraft of the Aces 25 – Bf 110 Zerstörer Aces of World War 2*, Osprey Publishing, Botley, 1999

WEBSTER, SIR CHARLES and FRANKLAND, NOBLE, *The Strategic Air Offensive against Germany 1939-1945, Volume I: Preparation*, HMSO, London, 1961

WIESINGER, GUNTER and SCHROEDER, WALTER, *Die Osterreichischen Ritterkreuzträger in der Luftwaffe 1939-45*, H Weishaupt Verlag, Graz, 1986

INDEX

References to illustrations are shown in **bold**. Plates are prefixed pl, with captions on the page in (brackets).

Adrian, Leutnant Ulrich 9
Albrecht, Hauptmann Egon 68
Angele, Unteroffizier Theodore 13

Bach, Oberfeldwebel Otto **46**, 48, **49**
Bacsila, Major Erwin 35, **44**, **82**
Bär, Major Heinz **45**, 45-6, **46**, 46, **47**, 48, 51, 52, 53, 90
Bauer, Feldwebel Konrad 'Pitt' pl**60**(94) 82, 90
Baunicke, Feldwebel 68
Beese, Oberleutnant Artur 20, 21, 35
Bendert, Oberleutnant Karl-Heinz 41
Bitsch, Hauptmann Emil 44
Blech, Flieger Georg 47, 48, 50-1
Boehm-Tettelbach, Major Karl 65
Boeing B-17 Flying Fortress 10, **13**, **15**, 24, **33**, 50, 66;
    defensive arcs **20**; 'MISS OUACHITA' **47**
Boesch, Feldwebel Oscar **35**
Böngen, Leutnant Ernst 19-30, **29**
Born, Gefreiter Heinrich 51
Bösch, Unteroffizier Oskar 72-3, **73**
Böttner, Unteroffizier Karl-Heinz pl**55**(92)
Brandl, Unteroffizier Gerhard 68
Bretschneider, Leutnant Klaus 80-1, 82
Brodbeck, Oberfeldwebel Kurt 49, 52
Brunner, Feldwebel Wolfgang 46
Buchholz, Feldwebel Fritz **79**
Buchner, Oberfeldwebel Hermann 88
Bühligen, Oberstleutnant Kurt 90
Burath, Oberleutnant Eberhard **46**, 46, 49

Clade, Leutnant Emil 32
Clausen, Hauptmann Erwin 23, 25
Consolidated B-24 Liberator 12, **75**, **80**;
    defensive arcs **28**

Dahl, Major Walther **39**, 66, 72, 75-6, **77**, 78-82, 90
Dassow, Leutnant Rudolf 91
Doppler, Leutnant Alwin 90
Dost, Leutnant Gerhard 39
Düllberg, Hauptmann Ernst **32**, 32

Eberle, Oberleutnant Friedrich **8**
Eder, Oberleutnant Georg-Peter 'Schorsch' **17**, 17, 43, 46, 47, 48, 49, 51, 52, 85, 90
Ehlers, Leutnant Hans 22-3, 25, 90
Engler, Unteroffizier Günther pl**61**(94)
Engst, Feldwebel Hubert 78
Erhardt, Feldwebel Otto **80**

Falkensamer, Hauptmann Egon **25**
Focke-Wulf Fw 190: **6**, 7, **9**, **12**, 13, **21**, **27**, **38**, **43**, **44**, **45**, **49**, 'Black 1' 52; pl**56**(92); 'Black 13' pl**60**(94);
    'Black 14' **73**; 'Blue 14' pl**60**(94) **72**; 'Brown 1' **54**(92);
    'Double Chevron' pl**56**(92); pl**60**(94); 'Double White Chevron' pl**54**(92); 'Red 3' pl**60**(94); 'Red 22' 47; 48;
    pl**57**(93); 'White 3' pl**59**(93); 'White 5' **81**; 'White 7'
    14; 'White 9' **70**; pl**60**(94) '**81**'; 'White 21'
    79; 'Yellow 2' **16**; 'Yellow 5' pl**60**(94) '92-3); 'Yellow 9'
    23; 'Yellow 13' **53**; 'Yellow 17' pl**59**(93) **76**
Franz, Oberleutnant Richard 34, **35**
Frey, Oberleutnant Hugo **18**, 18, 90
Frös, Oberfeldwebel Willi **68**, 68
Froschhauer, Unteroffizier Johann 51

Galland, Major Wilhelm-Ferdinand 22, **23**, 23
Galland, Oberst Adolf 8, 9, 11, 14, 24, 33, 71, 74, 75, 84
Gehr, Gefreiter Walter pl**56**(92)
Gerth, Leutnant Werner **35**; pl**60**(94) 73, 79, 90
Geyer, Hauptmann Horst **9**
Gillert, Oberfeldwebel 67
Glunz, Oberfeldwebel Adolf **37**, 37
Göring, Leutnant Peter 8
Graf, Major Hermann 24, 25
Gramberg, Oberleutnant Heinz-Dieter **83**
Grislawski, Hauptmann Alfred pl**55**(92) **70**, 70
Grob, Oberfeldwebel Artur 78

Gromotka, Oberfeldwebel Fritz 32-3
Grünberg, Oberleutnant Hans 'Specker' 88

Hackl, Hauptmann Anton 18: 42-3; **43**; pl**56**(92) 74, 90
Hagenah, Feldwebel Walter 72
Haugk, Hauptmann Helmut 93
Hermichen, Hauptmann Rolf-Günther 41-2, **42**, 90
Hirschfeld, Leutnant Ernst-Erich 78
Hofmann, Leutnant Wilhelm 35
Huppertz, Hauptmann Herbert 17, 36
Hutter, Oberfeldwebel Georg 51

Iffland, Leutnant Hans 71

Jansen, Feldwebel Arnold 53
Jenne, Hauptmann Peter **66**, 66, 91

Kahl, Feldwebel Heinz 47
Karch, Hauptmann Fritz 90
Kemethmüller, Oberfeldwebel Heinz 21
Kiel, Hauptmann Johannes 93
Kientsch, Oberleutnant Wilhelm 30-1, 90
Kirchmayr, Oberleutnant Rüdiger **46**; 46; 52; **53**; 53, pl**56**(92)
Klemm, Oberleutnant Rudolf 25-6
Koenig, Oberleutnant Hans-Heinrich 73-4, 90
Köhler, Hauptmann Armin 64
Köhne, Leutnant Walter 70
Kornatzki, Major Hans-Günther von **9**, 33, **35**, 43, 77
Kosse, Feldwebel Wolfgang 35, 43, **44**
Kupka, Gefreiter Hans **72**
Kutscha, Leutnant Herbert **27**

Lambertus, Unteroffizier Erich pl**59**(93)
Lang, Hauptmann Heinz **77**
Lang, Oberleutnant Emil 18
Langer, Hauptmann Karl-Heinz 76
Laskowski, Oberfeldwebel 42
Loos, Unteroffizier Walter pl**60**(94) **72**, 72, 90

Marburg, Oberfeldwebel Gerhard 35, **75**
Martini, Gefreiter Alfred **70**
Matoni, Major Walter **41**, 41
Maximowitz, Unteroffizier Willi **35**, 39, 82
Mayer, Hauptmann Egon 12-13: **13**; **14**; 14; pl**54**(92) 90
Mayer, Oberstleutnant Egon 38
Meissner, Hauptmann Hans 22
Messerschmitt Bf 109: 7, 9, **31**, **32**, **74**, **76**, 'Black 9' **39**;
    'Black 10' pl**54**(82); 'Black 12' pl**55**(92); 'Black
    Chevron' pl**54**(92); 'Double Black Chevron' pl**55**(92);
    'White 1' **8**, **25**; 'White 8' pl**59**(93); 'White 10'
    pl**55**(92); 'White 13' **72**; 'White 17' pl**59**(93); 'Yellow
    6' **cover**(4); pl**58**(93)
Messerschmitt Bf 110 Zerstörer 26, 62, **63**, **65**, **69**;
    '2N+EM' pl**57**(93); '3U+KR' pl**57**(93)
Messerschmitt Bf 210: 62, **63**; '2N+FR' pl**58**(93)
Messerschmitt Me 262: **84**, 84, 86; 'Green 1' **86**;
    'Green 3' pl**61**(94) 88; 'Green 4' pl**61**(94), 'White 7'
    pl**61**(94)
Messerschmitt Me 410: 62, **64**, 68; '3U+CC' pl**58**(93);
    '3U+LP' pl**58**(93)
Metz, Leutnant Rudolf 35, **44**, 77, **78**
Meyer, Hauptmann Karl-Heinz 11
Michalski, Major Gerhard 74-5
Mietusch, Hauptmann Klaus 21-2, **22**
Mölders, Oberst Werner 8
Moritz, Hauptmann Wilhelm pl**60**(94) 71, 73, **77**, 77, 79, 80
Moycis, Unteroffizier Rudolf 32
Müller, Leutnant Erich 87
Müller, Leutnant Siegfried **35**, 71
Müller, Major Friedrich-Karl 'Tutti' 71, 77, 90

Naumann, Hauptmann Johannes pl**54**(92)
Neumann, Leutnant Klaus **82**, 82
Niederreichholz, Feldwebel Kurt **46**, 47
Nowotny, Oberstleutnant Walter 84, 87

Oesau, Oberstleutnant Walter 'Gulle' **19**: 19; 37;
    pl**54**(92)

Olejnik, Hauptmann Robert 22

Palm, Feldwebel Albert **cover**(4): pl**58**(93)
Pfeiffer, Oberfähnrich 87
Piffer, Leutnant Anton-Rudolf 'Toni' 79, 90
Pingel, Hauptmann Rolf 9
Priller, Oberstleutnant Josef 22, 41

Quack, Leutnant Meinhard 47

Rademacher, Leutnant Rudolf **85**, 85, 87
Rammelt, Hauptmann Karl 31: pl**55**(92)
Remmer, Hauptmann Hans 74
Reschke, Feldwebel Willi 82, 90
Rödel, Oberstleutnant Gustav 75
Röhrich, Feldwebel Kurt **35**, 39, **44**
Rollwage, Oberfeldwebel Herbert 73, **74**, 76
Romm, Leutnant Oskar **82**, 82
Roth, Oberfeldwebel Willi 11
Rudorffer, Major Erich **89**, 89
Rüffler, Oberfeldwebel Helmut **72**, 72
Ruhl, Leutnant Franz 83; pl**55**(92)

Sauer, Feldwebel Max **47**
Schäfer, Feldwebel Hans 72
Schall, Leutnant Franz **84**, 84-5
Schild, Unteroffizier Jan 11
Schnörrer, Leutnant Karl 'Quax' **87**, 87
Schob, Hauptmann Herbert 91
Schroer, Major Werner **30**, 30, 90
Schuhmacher, Oberfeldwebel Leo **46**: **47**; 47; 48; 51,
    pl**57**(93)
Schulz, Unteroffizier Alfons 50
Schwarzenhölzer, Unteroffizier Helmut pl**55**(92)
Seeger, Oberleutnant Günther 'Hupatz' **31**, 31-2
Segatz, Hauptmann Hermann 45
Sievers, Unteroffizier Willi 67
Sommer, Oberleutnant Gerhard 24
Specht, Hauptmann Günther **25**, 25, 66
Spenner, Hauptmann Manfred 4
Staiger, Hauptmann Hermann **20**, 21, 90
Stamp, Major Gerhard 82-3
Stehle, Oberfeldwebel Fritz 68
Steiner, Feldwebel Franz **38**, 38
Steinhoff, Oberstleutnant Johannes 20, 28, 28-9, 45, 89
Stigler, Hauptmann Franz 30, **75**
Ströbele, Oberfeldwebel Georg 76
Sturm, Leutnant Gustav 88-9
Swoboda, Unteroffizier Hubert 49-50

Tichy, Oberleutnant Ekkehard 82
Tratt, Oberleutnant Eduard 63, **67**, 67
Triebel, Obergefreiter Werner 52

Unger, Leutnant Willi pl**59**(93) 71, 72, **76**, 79-80, 90

Vivroux, Unteroffizier Gerhard **44**: 44; pl**59**(93)
Vogt, Feldwebel Gerhard 70

Wahlfeld, Feldwebel Hermann 40, **44**
weapons: BK 5 5cm cannon **67**, 67-8; MG 151 20mm
    cannon **25**, **31**, 62, 73, **76**; MK 108 30mm cannon
    73, 84; R4M 55mm rocket **86**, 86; WGr 21cm
    underwing mortars **9**, **21**, **24**, **27**, **38**, **63**, 63-4,
    64, **65**, 66, **69**, 85, **86**, **88**
Weber, Unteroffizier Heinz 51
Weik, Leutnant Hans 71, 72, 90
Weissenberger, Major Theodore pl**61**(94)
Wennekers, Feldwebel Hans-Gerd pl**54**(92)
Werfft, Hauptmann Dr Peter **74**, 75
Wessling, Oberleutnant Otto 74
Willius, Leutnant Karl 'Charly' 40
Windisch, Oberfähnrich Walter 87
Wurmheller, Oberleutnant Josef **16**, 16-17, 90
Wurzer, Hauptmann Heinrich 78, 90

Zehart, Oberleutnant Othmar 34, **35**, 40
Zinkl, Unteroffizier 46, 47
Zweigart, Leutnant Eugen-Ludwig 40